Law Enforcement and the Paranormal

ZOLI ALTHEA BROWNE

D.Div, PhD, D.S.M., PhD

ISBN: 979-8-9902437-9-8

Dedication

My son, do not forget my law,
But let your heart keep my commands
For length of days and a long life,
And peace they will add to you.

Let not mercy and truth forsake you:
Bind them around your neck,
Write them upon the tablet of your heart,
And so find favor and self esteem
In the sight of God and man.

Trust in the Lord with all your heart,
And lean not on your own understanding;
In all your ways acknowledge Him,
And He shall direct your paths.
Proverbs 3:17

This thesis is dedicated to
Thomas Joseph Browne
1925-1993
Richmond, Ca. P. D.

Contents

THESIS STATEMENT

The body had floated for three days but had not sunk because it was not dead. No one knew. The evening dropped its drawers and mooned the day. Sunset broke open its wine bottle

crimson, letting spill its ecstatic vintage o'er the clear blue dress of the bay.

Things are rarely as they appear. The vantage point of perception is tainted by emotion and conditioning. How will you react when faced with the paranormal? This thesis addresses that concern. I propose to get you more comfortable with being uncomfortable. The world of the unseen is as unpredictable as the sense-laden reality we all share. Law enforcement professionals deserve to know what is

rarely spoken of, and what is always remembered in the privacy of your silence.

When I am told, "That stuff is a bunch of BS. I don't believe in it," my response is always, "Then what do you do when it happens?" Explaining away psi (Psychic

Issues and Phenomena) as a mental illness issue or a drug/alcohol issue won't cut it. Why? Because there is more to the unseen than what you can see, more than convenient labels from training. Fess up, now. You've all seen weird stuff, now, haven't you? Would you like to know more? When I asked an officer during a ride along, "What would you like to know about what I do?" his response was "Everything!"

This thesis was written for a PhD in Paranormal Research from Esoteric Interfaith Theological Seminary. A thesis is supposed to be a marriage of something I know well... my field of demonology and the paranormal, and an area I know little about. That is where

you enter the picture. Through my husband's work with SWAT and Spec. Opps, I have been honored to become family to many amazing cops and military personnel. All new to me. Being a recovering helpaholic (my term), I am driven to be of assistance and in service to my fellowman. As an ordained minister, ditto.

The purpose of my thesis on law enforcement and the paranormal is to arm you with intel about psi and to demonstrate that you are already prepared in ways you may not be aware. Those ways concern your ability to think clearly, assess a scene, gather concrete information, and protect yourself from harm. I also intend to create more awareness of what kinds of phenomena you could encounter and what to do about them. Fair enough? So, let's get the show on the road. Welcome to the

paranormal riding along with you on your journey of discovery.

From My Heart to Yours

Many years ago, I discerned that our greatest strengths could also be our greatest weaknesses. Cops have a strength of assessing physical data to make decisions appropriate for the circumstances in front of them. You are masters at recognizing change in our shared reality.  But when faced with an invisible enemy, this skill can at times hinder correct assessment and course of action due to your unfamiliarity with the stimuli.

Do I have any connection with law enforcement? My husband is a retired Special Opps Sergeant Major and former Tier One Operator. He is also the SWAT adviser  for a county in the northwest, and was given a Sheriff's commission to honor his skills, allowing him to train SWAT. The Sheriff of that county is a dear friend of ours. My father-in-law was a cop in Oakland, our nephew serves in San Pablo, and his dad is retired Chief in San Ramone. Most of our dearest friends and family members are cops. We were married by a SWAT cop

 and our best man was a sergeant in Washington state.

My knowledge and experience in Law Enforcement is minimal to say the least, yet my heart and mind are open and interested in this vast field of public service. I am

heartbroken to see and hear the abuses and defamations hurled

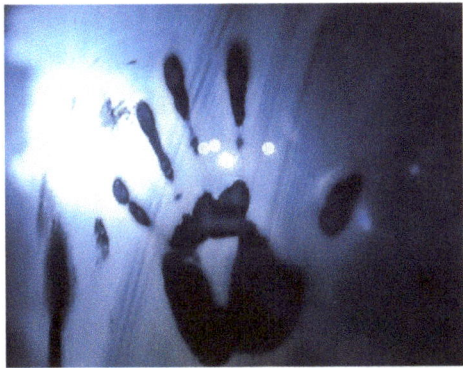 at cops from those who lack understanding of your daily personal sacrifices.

The field of paranormal research and investigation has expanded in the past several years as a response to public interest instigated by the plethora of TV shows and internet activity covering psi (psychic phenomena). A doorway to esoteric knowledge appears to have been opened to the masses.

Electronic methods of collecting and analyzing data have vastly improved parapsychological investigators' ability to

discern what's hiding under the bed. Numerous paranormal investigative groups now dot the map of our country, allowing access to assistance from those who fearlessly tread in the

footsteps of the unseen and usually unwanted. I stand in awe of their knowledge, humbled by their

courage and sense of adventure. Perhaps they are the ghost cops who can rid our shared reality of beings whose presence here is detrimental.

This thesis is a work of love and compassion for our brothers and sisters who wear the badge and keep us from harm. As an ordained minister my work involves caring for the wounded of spirit. Cops deserve to know what and why you are facing when confronted

with the unseen. Is it a discarnate spirit or demonic activity? Big difference there. Are you truly in danger or did you just get the wind knocked out you by a ghost who means no harm? I am certainly not claiming to be able to tell you exactly what happened, yet I CAN give you intel to begin to discern the nature of the phenomena.

There are no experts in the mysteries of life. But we can have expert knowledge. The mysteries are the art while parapsychology is the science. As an artist, I desire to create positive and accountable scenarios for cops to not only learn

from but to hopefully dialog more among yourselves. As a researcher and teacher, I teach from my personal experiences and learn from those of others. The greatest lesson in my forty years of working in the field is that anything is possible but not all is probable.

You simply cannot make up the truths that one encounters in the paranormal.

My hope and prayer are that this paper can alleviate suffering and shed much needed light on these peculiar events encountered by law enforcement. I have in no way covered the entire field of psi in this paper. It is simply too vast to do so. I have therefore included a bibliography of some of the best work available, as well as a section of prayers for Law Enforcement and your loved ones. My blessings go out to all who read this, with the aspiration of gifting knowledge to those who do so much in the face of danger.

Blessings from my heart to yours,

Zoli.

The Emotional Ghost

Is a ghost-spirit angry because of what happened when it was alive in a physical body? Is it possible to pass peacefully through the veil of time and space and raise the emotion of anger and vengeance from the other side? What about the emotions of concern and love?

Anything is possible, but all is not probable. The intrigue here points to the probability of creating human emotion from the Other Side. My experiences with human

spirits can attest to the fact that we certainly present our earthly personality even when dead.

My amazing father went through transition in April of 2012. He shows up at our home, still playful and concerned over our welfare. Dad appears to be thirty years old in his astral body, which is the form a bit finer in frequency than the physical body. The astral form allows all spirits to experience "life in their Heaven" (my quote) after physical death. Most look like they did around thirty years old, yet some prefer to keep their appearance at any other age so they can be recognized by the living. I am not speaking here of the demonic entities who have never been human, as the more powerful ones can appear as anything they want.

So, what is this astral realm and why do we go there after

death? In my forty years of research into the paranormal, I have

read varying and confusing explanations of exactly what these

seven levels are. Numerous esoteric texts explain the astral as

the frequency we assimilate to after shedding our physical form.

"Theosophy teaches
that when the physical body
dies the etheric body is left
behind and the soul forms
into an astral body on the
astral plane." (1)

"The psychical researcher F.W.H. Myers proposed the

existence of a metetherial world, which he wrote to be a world of images lying beyond the physical world. He wrote that apparitions have a real existence in the metetherial world which he describes as a dream-like state." (2)

"The astral plane, also known as the emotional plane is where consciousness goes after physical Earth. According to occult philosophy man possesses an astral body. The astral plane (also known as the astral world) was postulated by classical (particularly neo-Platonic), medieval, oriental and esoteric philosophies and mystery religions." (3)

"It is the world of the planetary spheres, crossed by the soul in its astral body on its way to being born and after death, and generally said to be populated by angels, spirits, or other immaterial beings." (4)

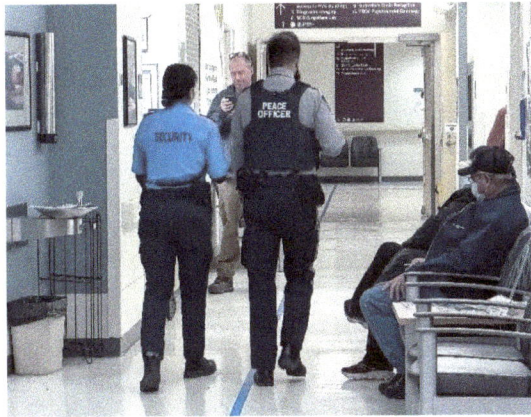

So, what does all this mean? When someone dies, they leave behind with those they knew, the impressions of their personality and deeds. After the body is dead, what is it that transfers awareness to another place, meaning the astral level? This very natural and automatic shift is like walking into a room and closing the door to find you cannot return through it. Is that scary to the recently deceased? Is the ghost emotional? It depends upon the personality of the deceased. As law enforcement professionals, you know that you will react

in stressful situations as well as you have trained. Reactions to shedding the body are similar in that response will depend on how much you practiced the understanding of the process.

What is it like? Loved ones and friends already in the astral meet the person and comfort, encourage, and guide him to join in the life in his heaven. It is helpful to prepare for this before death by understanding that the consciousness never dies...the shedding of the physical body is like releasing an egg from its shell. The outer is no longer needed. I highly encourage all people to learn

from their religious or spiritual teachings about the Other Side.

In the cases of suicide, murders, violent deaths, and sudden deaths, the spirit often crosses over only partially, due to confusion, fear, or another negative emotion. Whenever you are present at a fatality it's wise to protect yourself from whatever has died and whatever else has been attracted to the scene, ALWAYS if there is blood spilled. Like attracts like. Negative energies enter crime scenes and express as hostile feelings,

depression, anxiety, confusion, or plain old irritation. Crime scenes are confusing enough without having to deal with the Unseen polluting the area with negativity.

What about spirits like my dad who pass through the veil

with no trauma? It appears that these souls are the lucky ones, and yes, I believe in luck. Peaceful transitions can certainly produce hauntings if the deceased feels he has unfinished business. In Dad's case, he is aware that I am a medium and hyper sensitive to other-worldly phenomena. He seems to have no unfinished business, merely a fatherly desire to stay in communication whenever he can.

Why do I insist that we keep our emotions and the ability to create/express new ones after  death? My father continues to teach me about the after-death experience by demonstrating the human emotional expressions of irritation, impatience, joke-playing, questing for adventure, and issuing fatherly advice. Dad could repeat almost every joke he heard over his ninety-two years of living. He carried that love of laughter into his after-death life by showing me that he is still the same Marvin we all knew and

loved.

Ghosts of loved ones often manifest familiar cologne or other olfactory phenomena. They may create music you associate with them or whisper a loving thought in your ear. It appears that there is no limit to their creativity!

Thom and I moved into our Montana home several

months after Dad passed. His desire to see the home did not die with him, as he pulled a real "Marvin" on us only one week after settling in. I was in bed reading while Thom was in his office at the other end of the house. A loud crash from the dressing room yanked me out of bed, reminding me later of the "bowling ball drop" that spirit can create to get attention. I shot out of bed and almost ran into Thom as he hurried through the darkened dressing room that separates our bedroom from the main house.

"What the hell was that?!" we both exclaimed.

"I thought you slammed a door," Thom continued.

We did a perimeter search of the upstairs before concluding that nothing was broken or broken into. But then I had an image of Dad giggling like a schoolgirl, standing to the side of me with his hands covering his mouth.

"They told me I could do that," he began. "That was SO much fun!"

By then I was laughing but still shaken. I saw him standing in front of me with three of his buddies from Camp

Horseshoe, c.a. 1938. They were all laughing hysterically and I was getting pissed-off.

"Don't DO that, you guys! You scared the hell out of us!" I exclaimed as I saw their forms begin a decay pattern.

Anyone who knew Marvin would recognize this signature of his personality. So

much for the image I erroneously had of him as a wise calm being floating in his Heaven. Over the past several years he as continued to play pranks on me but also to show up just to make sure I am OK.

One month after the bowling ball event, I was in the garage unpacking boxes. I looked up because I sensed his

presence and saw him gazing at the contents of what I had already unpacked. "Hey, Dad," I began. "What are you up to now?" I teased.

"I just came to check on you," he replied.

"I'm doing fine, Dad. You don't have to keep checking if I am all right. I want you to enjoy your time over there and focus on what else you are doing. Really, I'm great."

He got up from the bench he was sitting on and gave me that compassionate smile he was so known for.

"Sweetie, love never dies, you know. It never ends."

I barely saw him dematerialize from the tears welling up in my eyes. Got it, Dad. Love does that.

So, what about the other side of the spectrum, do angry spirits pass over in that state and haunt their own memories? Can a dead person develop insanity on the other side? I have not come across any of this in my research, but I will deduce that it is indeed a possibility to create new emotions in the astral realm

as well. My bet would be that insanity lives on in the ghost...as above, so below. There are  hospitals and healing centers on the other side to deal with this. Ghost-spirits with an agenda usually project an emotion connecting them to their manifestation. If Aunt Peggy died before her daughter could make it to the emergency room, Aunt Peggy passed over with unfinished business.

When you roll on a fatality, that person probably passed  over in a state of trauma and shock. That spirit has an agenda. When a drugged-out dealer holding his girlfriend hostage and is taken out by SWAT, that guy passed over with an agenda.

Drug and alcohol-involved homicides, suicides, or fatalities of other sorts ALL pass over with the agenda of still craving the addiction that swallowed their soul during their life on earth. Discarnate beings swarm around these cases like flies on syrup in August.

If you feel "something weird," you can be sure that nasty ghosts are trying to enter a body and influence it to use or abuse substances. Pay attention to your intuition. If you yourself have alcohol, drug,

gambling, or sexual addictions I would encourage you to get right with God because you are absolutely at risk in the presence of these beings. There are more discarnate addicts in bars, hospitals, and jails than the living who inhabit those places.

Blood. Why does blood at a scene attract beings who are similar to the one whose blood is now on the street? Think about it. Blood is the life  force. About 15 percent of the human form is composed of blood. An exsanguinated body will spill about two to three gallons on the ground. That is the magnetic signature of the person. Iron is the magnetic mineral that will attract discarnate beings to the spot where the blood spilled. Blood contains the life force. Wow. The corpse itself loses

interest after the blood is gone. And what if that blood remains in the soil, on the wooden floor, or on the bottom of the pond? Does it ever really disintegrate energetically? No. There, you have the emotions of the past still present in the now. This is why you will feel weird

around blood or places that have been soaked with death.

I used to investigate haunts and assist in dislodging unwanted otherworldly interlopers from homes. When I lived in Nashville I recall wandering around the Civil War battlefield. The air was so thick you could slap it and it would just laugh at you. The magnetic residue of emotion coupled with the blood- soaked soil simply oozed with the signature of pain and death. Why would the dead not have emotion when humanity itself is fueled with it? A bit of explaining on my part is called for.

I began this section of my thesis with that assumption. To prove it may take some doing. Why?

The paranormal has no experts. The mysteries of life are indeed inexplicable until the time when they are, well,

explained. We can have expert knowledge but no experts. The emotions of ghosts should be dignified with the curiosity of exactly how a non-physical being lacking a neural network and nerve endings can actually feel. Does the astral body replicate the physical? Metaphysical knowledge claims that it does, that the astral form is exactly like the physical except of a higher

vibration. That would explain why certain cultures "feed hungry ghosts." But do ghosts poop?!

The emotional ghost appears then to replicate its personality after it is dead. New emotions CAN be created after death because consciousness is not dependent upon the physical body. What generates the emotions? Desire and Will projected as response to stimuli specific to the astral plane. That plane also has an exact replica of the one we know as physical. A discarnate may not recognize he is dead because his world looks exactly as it did when he was alive. Give this some thought. We will address other ghostly issues later on, but in the next section want to give you a bit of background on yours truly.

My Story

I was born in the last century in a southern city ripe with ghosts, crime, and rich beauty. The city of New Orleans was built upon the assumption that anything is possible, that is, if you dare challenge the dark powers of the Unseen.

I was born smack in the middle of New Orleans in Touro Infirmary. The government of Louisiana was still under Napoleonic Law, so the birth records were sealed until a half  century later when Mary Ellen (my favorite private eye), found them and revealed to me the hidden pieces.

But why am I telling you this? For a good reason: the

blood, aromas, and psychic aura of New Orleans still course through my veins. I am a GRIT...a girl raised in the south. What has influenced my life even more is the sensual and phenomena-laden part of me that is hooked in to that city. Hard to explain rationally, but you get it...I know you do.

Everything of this world has a beginning, a middle, and an end. We love and lose, cry, and laugh, dancing between the emotional poles of one end of it or another. The point is, we all share many of the same experiences. That is how we relate. But if we isolate and begin to delude ourselves that our problem is unique, that is when the icky stuff can float in. We are social creatures, created to give and get the best and the worst.

This thesis will inform you how to relate to fellow officers, friends, and family when (not if) you encounter the paranormal.

I live with this 24/7. I don't know why I was gifted with the ability to see and talk to dead folks...to know what will happen if you go down a certain path, to literally see Gnomes and Faeries, to empathize and connect so deeply with others that the pain and joy can overwhelm me for hours. Dunno. But I do know it all began when I was about nine years old.

We lived in a community about thirty minutes out of the

city of Birmingham, Alabama. Our ten acres of hardwoods and dogwoods allowed me plenty of space to build forts, talk to the little people and then make the mistake of telling people about it. The fort thing did not bother them but the Faery talks did not go over well. Other kids hated me and I was always the scapegoat and the kid left out of games at school. God wanted me to learn to be alone but not lonely, and to learn compassion and tolerance for others before my warrior spirit could take over.

And then there was the Autism thing. In the 1950s in

Alabama, not much brilliant medical intel got through the sultry fog of complacency. My poor parents were

horribly frustrated that their weird little daughter could not learn in school even though her IQ tested off the charts. I floundered until age thirty-five to communicate with others and just

recently learned to make and hold eye contact. I could see thoughts floating above people's heads, and many of those thoughts were not what was coming out of their mouth. In southern society it is NOT polite to call another a liar. So, I learned that the graphs I saw above others heads were to be kept within. Somehow, I knew God had a plan for me, so I let my gifts unfold.

Are you getting the picture? I knew you would. Paranormal phenomena have been my constant companion for over 60 years. I want you to benefit from some of what I have learned so that you can inform others, deal? Everyone is born with the ability to discern phenomena, but most fluff it off as "just my imagination," so don't do that! If your kid sees something,

hears something, or wants you to know about "something," it is child abuse to tell him it is just his imagination. Gut-up and listen because he has nowhere else to go with that anxiety. You are not making him feel better by being a dumb adult and trying

to convince him nothing happened that he just saw. Get It?

There is an old Chinese aphorism that says, "the truth is not fine sounding." Harsh realities create strong personalities. As a native of New Orleans,

I can assure you that there is much more going on than your physical senses can

detect. But you secretly knew that, didn't you? When it is our children telling those hard truths, the grace of innocence becomes our teacher. Our own kid within is always aware, challenging its adult self to see the world with the eyes of a child. Christ asks us to be as little children to enter the Kingdom of Heaven. All is within God's world, even evil is allowed as part of The Plan. We can simply follow the prompts and intend

 to do good work. I don't think God ever asks anyone when they get to Heaven if they were

a successful businessman or what size jeans they wore. I would like to imagine He asks for an accounting of how we treated ourselves and others. From the accounts of those I speak to on the other side, heaven IS heaven. The more aware you are about the unseen part of God's world; the greater will be your talent in navigating what is visible. So, go do good works!

SERVE ✫ HONOR ✫ PROTECT

Phenomena

Of all the questions I have been and am currently asked, most refer to the phenomena you encounter during a paranormal event: What was it? Where did it come from? Why was it there? Was it malicious in its intent?

My response to any of these or similar concerns inevitably relates to the environment in which you find yourself during the encounter. Environment is everything. Why? Just as with humans in a scene investigation, Spirit or demonic

beings leave imprints I call SIGNATURES. As with your

investigations,

paranormal work

seeks clues and

trace evidence

defining intent and behavior. These can be recognized either

from the emotional impact the encounter has on your nervous

system, electromagnetic signatures captured on

parapsychological meters, the disruption of physical objects

during the encounter, or other unusual signals imprinting upon

your senses, either physical or intuitive.

What kind of phenomena might you encounter? Several

I would like to mention are orbs, vocalizations, and the

manifestations of lowered

temperature.

Orbs are floating

balls of luminous

electromagnetic substance.

They are usually colorless while swirling or flashing sparks can radiate from or around them. They are called orbs because they are balls of light. Some may be colorful but most appear rather clear or clouded. What are orbs and why do you see them? Orbs are believed to be electromagnetic transport systems for spirit or demonic beings. The orb is formed from thoughts or energies

projected by non-physical beings for the purpose of allowing them to manifest. When the energy dissipates from the orb, the being is no longer able to use that transport to manifest. Why would you see one? Because the being wants you to, usually. It may not even know you are present. What should you do? I would suggest avoiding its path and carefully monitoring your intuition and emotional reaction. Orb transports can carry healing or malicious entities. There is no way I can advise your response because every encounter will be different. Why? Because the encounter will be specific to the environment in which you find yourself.

Vocalizations are communications from the other side

that manifest as auditory signatures. Why might you hear them? Again, the being may be attempting to garner your attention, but you may simply have encountered a rip in the veil in between the physical and the etheric worlds. How can you discern a pattern? The environment in which you find yourself will allow clues as to the reason for and why it is occurring. How is that possible if you have never heard anything like this before? Use your

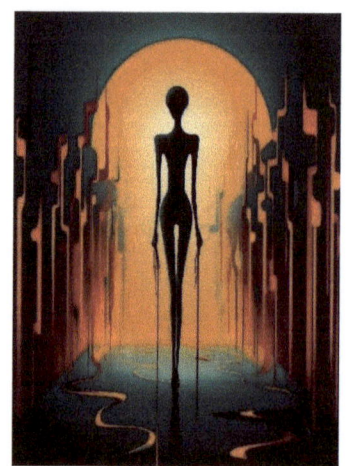

training to collect informative data as to what you know about the area, the people involved, its history and any issues surrounding the phenomena. Does the voice or its message seem

familiar to you? A spirit may indeed be trying to contact you, but be on the alert that demonic beings can con and deceive you as they mimic loved ones with intel only you may know. Again, use caution and be discerning. Trust your gut because a child's voice often does not come from a child in demonic settings.

Have you ever walked into a space and felt the temperature drop with no apparent reason? Perhaps you have

felt a cold wind move through you in a closed room. Spirit as well as demonic entities suck up all the warmth in the room as they attempt to manifest or create phenomena. Their electromagnetic field

absorbs, so to speak, the energy of heat which donates to their ability to scare the holy hell out of you. Even though it may be

Aunt Betty saying hello, it may also be a discarnate who hangs

out at the location, or even a

demonic being creating

havoc.

Believe it or not, some of the coolest education you can

access are the plethora of spooky shows currently on T.V. The

paranormal investigators put a lot of time and energy into

passionately discerning the differences in paranormal

phenomena. My favorite is *The Dead Zone,* with an amazing

psychic and retired cop. Way cool. Even though these shows are

created for a TV audience,

heavily produced and laden

with emotional drama, you

can actually learn a lot from

the work of these groups.

Some are better than others,

but that's nothing new, is it?

So, what about the truly demonic stuff? I have addressed

elsewhere in this thesis the absolute importance of cleaning up

your lifestyle and emotional thoughts. The demonic feed off of the seven deadly sins and lap up your negative reactions to their evil activity. Numerous wonderful books are available to educate you on the types of entities and their signatures. I have listed them in the back of this thesis and encourage you to read the ones that spark your interest. My intent here is to offer you a hand in friendship, not to list hundreds of names of demons and angels. But again, pay attention to your gut reactions while employing the same skills you use in the field to the paranormal.

Measuring The Environment

Control over your environment is primary, first cause, right? What happens when you cannot get a good read on what's up? How do you control what you have not been trained to encounter? Enter electromagnetic testing devices. Way cool. Paranormal investigators use these things to read signatures of

temperature changes, sudden battery loss, creepy feelings that something is THERE but you can't see it, and otherworldly phenomena you only seem to see on TV...happening to some poor fool in a slasher movie.

Well, move over paranormal dudes because now many of these

devices can be
found with your
friend Google.

So, what
are these things
that measure time

and space doing a wacky dance? Spirit energy is

electromagnetic and rather easy to discern. I will tell you about

several devices that you can keep in your cruiser or in your

bag...not expensive and more common than handcuffs. First, a

35 mm camera. It is known that you can sometimes take some

shots of a seemingly empty room that some

phenomena has visited and voila, a shadow

person, an orb, or a something else shows

up in your photo. The visible spectrum is

pitifully narrow compared to what is

measurable by your camera. Use 400 film

and be patient. A digital camera is also valuable and you can see the activity right away with that.

A motion sensor will indicate activity when a ghost or being is active in front of it. Pretty cool. What about  a barometer? Changes in barometric pressure often accompany paranormal activity. A digital recorder can pick up sounds in your environment, especially if there is known activity. You really never know what is going to be useful unless you get creative and just try combining some of these measuring devices.

 Of course, a video camera is easy to use and can reveal lots of finds. Digital thermometers are another easy find and they can indicate temperature change in cold or hot spots.

Some of the less common but highly useful devices include: Digital EMF Meter, which measures the

electromagnetic signatures of the environment you are testing. Ghosts and Beings create surges in the electromagnetic spectrum when they appear. What about a Spirit Box? Now that's an amazing device! The P-SB7 Spirit Box detects spirit vocalizations using radio frequencies. Names, complete sentences, whole conversations between one spirit and another have all been picked up and recorded on this devise...truly a doorway to the next level.

So, now that you are aware that spirits can communicate with you using radio waves, magnetic fields,

microwaves as well as static charge shifts, you are more prepared to do battle with the unseen. Cops are usually first responders so don't miss out on the opportunity to capture some great intel from the world of the unseen. You can make visible and audible what was unrecordable just a few years ago. It's an amazing field to capture on camera or with a measuring device. I highly encourage you to peruse the Internet sites of the dozens of paranormal teams who make amazing discoveries in the field.

Measuring Your Courageous Will

All right. You now have some tools to choose from. What are you going to do if the spooky stuff does not fit into the MI, drug-induced, natural phenomena, or I-always-roll-on-this categories? Feel free to get the hell out if you are up against demonic and truly evil stuff emanating from the unseen. Law enforcement already deals with enough human evil to allow you to read that signature. Most of the paranormal events you will encounter will involve hauntings of people, places, or objects. Yes, objects can be haunted. What does that mean?

Sometimes a curse has been placed on a material object, or perhaps its previously alive owner was so  attached to it that he did not get the e-mail that, dude, you're done. There are several ways for you to deal with that scenario. Did you pick up an object or brush by something that gave you the willies? Do NOT ignore that intuitive hit. Transference of ickiness can occur if the thing is cursed and looking for a new blood bag host. And don't touch that. If you look at an object or if perhaps a homeowner reveals that "weird stuff always happens around this and oh, yeah, it moves itself at night,"  believe it. Don't go all Arnold on me and challenge the object or the statement. If you are required to collect and bag the thing, wear gloves, and wash your hands after even handling it.

What about hauntings of places? That's more common because walls CAN talk. Everything material gives off

electromagnetic signatures of what has occurred in and around it. Time does not affect space in this instance...if it occurred in 1776 the signature is as fresh as if it happened ten minutes ago. Really. That is why when you walk into any building or room it can feel different from the space you just exited. That's a no-braincr, so common and wired into our experience that we rarely think about it. Unless, of course, the signature is so intense that it registers on the lower end of the spectrum which approaches physical manifestation. That is

when and where you will experience the paranormal without your ghost meters. Pay

attention to this. Gals are more tuned into these signals than guys. Intuition is more of a feminine thingy, but Gavin de

Becker tells men to GO THERE and recognize that intuitive side within. You get the point.

Let's look at some possible scenarios and ways to deal with them...

First: You roll on a late night call for "suspicious activity" at an address you all have memorized. For the third time this month the mom has requested help because "whenever the kids go into the back room, they run out screaming that the man is back." You check it out and, as usual, no one is there...at least no one is visible.

So, no crime has been committed, everyone is safe by your standards, and you tell them to "have the room checked out maybe by an electrician or a contractor and have a nice night." But as you walk toward the front door the little boy walks up and says "There really is a bad man in there but no one will believe me. He hurts me sometimes," while he's pointing to hand bruises on his arm. Red flag. You look at the parents who say this is news to them. The two older sisters say "Yeah, we quit telling you guys because you never believe us and said we were lying," then shyly

reveal some pretty awful stuff that has gone on in that room when the parents were clearly asleep or not at home. They say that the room smells really bad sometimes and they hear a baby crying but cannot find where it might be coming from, that it all started when they moved in last month and would hear three

knocks on the wall, usually around 2:30 or 3:00 AM. The parents never heard any of this.

What is going on? You suspect someone is lying and someone else is in on it to get attention. After all, those kids are in a new school with no new friends. The family seems normal enough, but as the kids continue to emotionally reveal more awful stuff to two visibly

shaken and stunned parents, a warranted anxiety creeps into your mind that maybe, just maybe, this is one of "those" calls you just need to get away from. Too weird.

Everything I just created in that scenario has the signature of a demonic attack. Let me tell you why: The

demonic often goes after the weakest and most vulnerable ones while making sure the powerful

ones, meaning in this case the parents, are left out of it so they will believe nothing is happening, see? And that is truly awful to do to a child, but the demonic hate you and everyone with a soul. What about the timing? Jesus Christ was crucified at 3:00

in the afternoon, so the demonic will make fun of that by doing evil at 3:00 in the morning. They are also insulting the Holy Trinity. They have no original thought so they do the opposite of what good represents. Demons are stupid and tediously perverted in that they have no free will and no ability to grow or change. Truly, they are boring and uncreative.

Demonic entities send in the really stupid, low-level ones before the more dangerous demons come in if the attack moves from Infestation to the Oppression stage. More on that later. They feed off of negative emotions. They want to create discord and cause you to worry that you are going crazy. One of their goals is to isolate you so that will feel

hopeless and give in to raw negative emotions. Just think of the movie … alone in that isolated place with no one but their own fertile imaginations to play with.

Terrible smells often accompany demonic attack. Feces or sulfur is common. A room can stink like an open sewer and then be cleared in an instant. Looking for the source is what the demonic tricks you into doing. In exorcisms when the big guns have possessed someone and the devil or demon is talking back to the priest, they have been known to say "In a future time we

will bow down to your God...but not today!" Those raps on the wall are one of the signatures for the first stage of an attack. Let me quote here the stages of demonic activity from NYC cop and paranormal investigator Ralph Sarchie. "Infestation is an external assault: it causes physical phenomena as the demonic manipulates objects. Oppression has two parts: while the outward manifestations continue and intensify there is also a more sinister aspect that's not visible to the eye. Infestation affects the physical house; oppression goes beyond and "haunts those who live there." (1)

Do you recall that the family in question had recently moved into this house? It appears that the house or land it is on or surrounded by is under demonic attack. This poor family rented a house in hell. If they moved, perhaps their issues with demonic stuff would end. But did they bring it with them or did one of them do some activity that magnetized evil to them all? This would take some questioning on the part of a paranormal team. And that gets us to the point that I want you

to consider...either leave the situation alone or call in a paranormal investigator. The internet hosts sites of more than a few groups, at least one of which will be near you or perhaps willing to travel to a meet

 and greet with the unholy. Yes, some of them charge for their work and time but many do not. Why not collect a few names and pass that on to the afflicted family? Who knows, you might be saving a family or a life. I guess it depends on how much time you want to put into this, but I have to assume that if you are reading this you have at least a passing interest in the paranormal.

Officer Sarchie also says,  "You can sense evil: Your whole body responds to it. The demonic know how to create the maximum amount of terror in each person, because they know your weaknesses...I don't consider myself a psychic proper, but it's an unnatural feeling that your senses. A lot of people describe it as an eerie or creepy feeling that something is terribly

wrong." (2)

What behavior attracts demons or negative beings? Never, NEVER use a Ouija

Board. It is an open door to the lower Astral levels where these

entities wait to be called into service. And that type of service

can open Pandora's Box. Dedicating yourself to Satan, even as

a cute little test to see what will happen, is beyond stupid. But

people do it anyway. God is always listening but so is the

demonic. Using any sort of divinatory cards or devices to

control or harm another is a no-no. Curses exits also. Every word

we say is recorded by one side or the other, so learning to watch

our tongue can mean the difference between a great life and one beset with "bad luck." Calling

in negative Beings or tempting the demonic is not wise. Also,

never burn a cursed object or a Ouija Board...weigh it down and drown it in a deep body of water so that no one can find it Why

not just burn it and let the ashes be carried

off by the four winds? Fire and dry

conditions are connected with masculine

power in a way that will not return the

object to any safe elemental form. Water

is yin, feminine and absorbs the energy in

such a way that it is not dissipated in ashes and once again

available for reassembling in a different form.

Beliefs about what is evil, who is evil, and what attracts

it will differ from one culture and religion to the next. There are

many fundamentalist people who believe that any sort of

divination is evil, as is Halloween and Goth clothing. Whatever.

(Better get rid of my leather

biker stuff). In my world,

the only sin is Hate and all

its nasty little cousins,

which includes heavy

judgment on others' beliefs. Some of the most ethical folks I know are Wiccan.

I have two ministerial ordinations from The Esoteric Interfaith Seminary, one from The University of Metaphysical Sciences, as well as two Masters degrees, and four PhDs. S-o-o-o, I guess I do have some authority to assure you that your beliefs are sacred to you and precious as long as First Do No Harm is included in your code of ethics. Enough said.

This thesis is in no way inclusive of everything I would like Law Enforcement to know to better arm you in your walk on the wild side. You see about everything there is to see, and I know absolutely that you just

can't make up some of the stuff that happens.

One of my husband's famous statements is, "The more

you know, the less you

need." Even though he

applies that to hunting

and extreme situations

in the wilderness, I find

it applies well to your work. Why? The more you train, work-

out, do situational awareness trainings and visualizations, the

better equipped you will be when faced with the real thing.

Similarly, the more you know about the paranormal the less you

will need to waste precious seconds in anxiety, confusion, or

disruption of safety. Your ability to assess and control your

environment will be maximized when you minimize ignorance.

Don't ever take for granted the power of the moment, to act

confidently and intelligently around a paranormal event. Wasting time in fear gives the other side the advantage.

But wait, what IS fear? Gavin De Becker has as awesome take on this:

"True fear is a signal in the presence of danger. It is always based on something we perceive, something in our environment or our circumstances. Unwarranted fear is always based on our memory or our imagination." (3)

So, true fear is reactive emotional responding to a person, place, or thing, which includes a paranormal encounter.

How you will react is determined by your training, your mind set and your emotions at the time of the encounter.

Then what is it that you are feeling when you wonder what the hell IT was you met in the basement? No real threat is

present but you don't feel good about the situation? That is called anxiety, so you can scratch off the idea that you lay awake feeling afraid of anything. "Anxiety is caused ultimately, by predictions in which you have little confidence...predictions in which you have high confidence free you to respond, prepare, adjust, accept, feel sadness, or do whatever is needed. Accordingly, anxiety is reduced by improving the quality of your predictions...certainty is the antidote to anxiety." (4) Arm your confidence with information on the paranormal to reduce anxiety.

Then there is anxiety's partner called worry. "Worry is a way to avoid change; when we worry, we don't do anything

about the matter...worrying feels like we are doing something...worrying is a way to rehearse dreaded outcomes so that if they occur, the worrier believes he will be more prepared." (5)

Why worry? It can be a habitual addiction as can anxiety. As a law enforcement professional, you owe it to yourself to level out the emotional field and adapting to war-like circumstances with healthful alternatives. You can over drink, over medicate, over anything until the karma train rolls into the station and you are forced to change from the outside, rather than adjust and learn calming techniques from within. Do WHAT?! Try meditation. You don't have to out yourself to anyone else and you will be amazed at the end result.

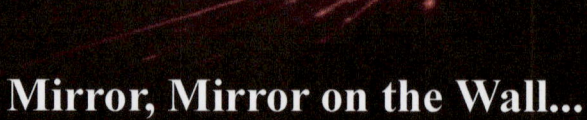

Mirror, Mirror on the Wall...

Contact with the demonic can mirror your own unresolved fears. Hate imbalances the kindest soul and disrupts relationships with self as well as with others. Never underestimate the power of your own unresolved issues hiding behind the shield of addiction, blame, self-loathing, and any other negative energy. This is not the power you want to project.

The Judeo-Christian society of our great country recognizes the power of repentance and forgiveness. During the Jewish

High Holy Days, in between Rosh Hashanah (the Jewish New Year by their calendar) and Yom Kippur (the Day of

Repentance), those practicing the Jewish faith are asked to spend time reviewing their deeds during the previous year. On Yom Kippur, the holiest day of the year, they are expected to fast from sundown the evening before (all Jewish holy days commence then), and spend the day in temple before breaking fast at sundown.

For Catholics, the act of repentance can involve going to

confession and perhaps a daily asking of God to "remove my shortcomings." The Lord's Prayer is communally said as well as prayed all over the world in the sanctity of one's own prayer time. To "forgive us our trespasses as we forgive others" is a prayer of grace. Any time you humble yourself to reflect on harmful words and deeds, followed by a prayer of forgiveness,

you fall under the protection

of the Holy Spirit Who is

available for anyone of any

faith. "Ask and ye shall

receive...." Christianity in

all its denominations holds fast to the doctrine of forgiveness

and grace.

When Gautama Buddha sat under the Bodhi tree and

was accosted with the illusions of the material world, his test

was to recognize the demonic falsehoods and choose love over

fear.

When Jesus was tested

in the Garden of Gethsemane,

Satanic forces tempted him

with the pleasures and

temptations of this world. His test was the same, to maintain

frequency above that of temptation and satanic powers. These

same tests are presented to you and I on a daily basis...maybe not as extreme, but the choice is still there. Can you be strong enough to resist what you know or even suspect is wrong, and stand on moral high ground when no one else is around?

In religious writings, gardens pose an interesting problem. The Garden of Eden began as a place of perfect peace

and then, well, you know the rest. Then there was The Garden of Gethsemane—same story. Perhaps the lesson is not to be fooled by the earthly illusion of beauty and perfection because trouble is right around the corner.

Why is this so essential in police work? Officers see the worst of the worst. When at work you rarely think your shift will be calm and serene. You are warriors, readying for battle. The more Spiritual Armor you can wear, the greater your power is to fight whatever is out there. The demonic hates you and will

attack your weaknesses and unresolved, hidden traits. Start NOW to find a spiritual path to comfort and protect you 24/7.

In the foreword to the amazing book *Spiritual Survival for Law Enforcement*, Sergeant Craig Hunter explains the mind, body and spiritual readiness required for cops in your training as well as during your career. He validates the work done by the Critical Incident Stress Foundation and the Fraternal Order of Police in helping those in crisis to return to health and a sense of well being in emotional and mental health. Sergeant Hunter

continues to address these needs to include spiritual health and healing from trauma:

"When thinking of the whole person as made up of three equal parts, physical, mental and spiritual, effort must be made to maintain each arena of life to ensure complete health." (1)

God created you to enjoy a full life with a sense of security and a vibrant expectancy for goodness in your future. But the extreme stress of your chosen profession challenges that very ideal. I urge all of you to do some serious soul-searching

and value the paths open to you. Sergeant Hunter admits that most cops ignore the inevitable topic of their eventual demise, partially out of not wanting to discuss it with other cops and also trying to ignore an unpleasant reality.

"When the job is over, either through retirement, resignation or critical incident, everything can fall apart in an instant. You need a strong safety net of faith to catch you.

Without that safety net all can seem hopeless, a feeling that can be fatal. You are too important to feel hopeless." (2)

For this thesis, I am unqualified to know what you think or feel when you roll on a call or respond to a terrible scene. But I am absolutely qualified to listen to your stories, hear incident reactions from your loved ones, and at least try to make some sense of the horrors you file away as unmentionable or

unresolvable. This is where your relationship with God can help you, by trusting that you are only as alone as you want to be and by admitting that every one of your brothers carry the burden of similar wounds. To courageously reach out your hand in friendship and lend a compassionate ear to a brother or sister on the force could be a life saver for you both. Somebody has to start. Someone has to create greater

 dialog among law enforcement, so why not you? You may be pleasantly surprised at the reaction you get from a cop whom you are sure would never discuss his spiritual beliefs or even the paranormal events he has encountered.

"There is a fundamental difference between one who performs the job of law enforcement (internally oriented) and one who performs the same job 'externally oriented'. When one does what one does from a place of inner clarity of purpose, from an internally defined sense of purpose, the career has much to offer in the way of satisfaction and development of character. The work will be nourishing and fulfilling, and it will contribute to a further refinement of character, in accordance with the principle that 'We are made kind by being kind.' (Hoffer)." (3)

Like does attract like, so what do you really have to lose by reaching out in kindness and suggesting that you are willing to listen to a brother or sister's fears in facing a paranormal event? Miracles happen all the time, yet we dismiss them as something happening to the other guy. Never forget that you are God's perfect creation. You are a specialist on a mission from the Great Beyond. Make the most of it by looking deeply into the mirror of self, facing your demons, and courageously creating a spiritual path for yourself. You deserve it! Not everything "happens for a reason" but you can make reason out of what happens. I bless your journey and hold you in my heart as warriors doing God's Will to protect and serve.

That Thing Called Death

"The fear of dying is one of the greatest fears of life. People are afraid of illness, of being ill, afraid of getting old, afraid of dying, of death. These are the 3 major fears shared by all humanity. Some people are not afraid of illness; they have never been ill and are not afraid of getting ill. But most are people who are totally dominated by the fear of being ill. And there are the professionally- ill people who are always ill because that brings the kind of attention that they did not get from their mother. The sad

thing is that you can be afraid of dying, afraid of being ill, and afraid of getting old all at once. These 3 fears dominate the lives

of many people." (1)

Do we leave this earth with these same worries and fears? Is this one of the reasons ghosts haunt—are they still trying to resolve unfinished business in a stasis of fear? I believe it is. If you refer to the section in this thesis, THE EMOTIONAL GHOST, you can see how emotions trap us and hold us hostage to the past. If a ghost is hanging around, trying to reclaim, relive and/or resolve emotions from the past, it can go on ad nauseum until someone releases it. Who-you-gonna call?

Paranormal investigators, spiritual and religious folks, as well as perhaps yourself are

willing to inform a spirit that their dance card is full and it is time to move into their future. I would advise against dancing with the dead unless your confidence and knowledge exceeds your anxiety around dealing with them. Why? In my experience I can rarely be absolutely positive that the benign ghost is who  they say they are or appear to be. Arm yourself before hand by reading up on these issues and perhaps befriending some of the folks who do this work.

But back to the death thing. We fear being out of control around the unknown. Another human trait, "It is mainly to do with the notion that time exists. If they knew that out of the physical body they will experience a vividness, an intensity of life, which they have never known on the physical plane, they would not have that fear of being dead." (2)

So, don't ghosts feel this wonder? Not if they have one foot on the other side and one still stuck here. We humans are unaware of the truth that we are eternal, all that dies is the physical body, our minds are still alive if not more so when we shed the body.

"For those who sense themselves to be at the center of the

universe, everything they hear, feel, everything they experience has to go through them. There is no sense of objectivity. There is no 'out there'. There is no 'other'. Everything has to be passed through themselves in order to be realized at all...it is the cause of all our anxiety, our conflict, our unhappiness, our inability to live life in a full, adequate way." (3)

In this next section, I will give you some prayers that I wrote for you, along with some oldie-but- goodies from religious texts. I chose to write this in a new font so that you can

recognize them as having a different feeling than the rest of the thesis. I hope they bring you comfort and encourage you to focus on fortifying your spiritual weaponry for the daily battles you all fight.

Blessings and Prayers

What do you believe and what do you believe in? Perhaps you have encountered some things that caused your beliefs to change.

"The kingdom of heaven lies within. Each and every human being is endowed with the love, light, and power of the Creator. That triune blessing lives inside of You have perfect access to the God within simply by asking.

To ask is to open the golden door leading to the

heart Where do you begin? Perhaps you were raised in a religious practice which has remained comforting to you.

Maybe you found one more suitable, or maybe that is simply not something you like.

My Sergeant Major husband claims, "There are no atheists on the battlefield." Are there atheists (non believers in Higher Power) in the presence of the paranormal? It appears we are all hard-wired to believe in Something. What that Something is should be between you and your Higher Power. It knows you

and what you believe even before you can speak it.

That should be a comfort, but if you are not comfortable with the invisible Creator, how will you deal with the invisible paranormal?! What about getting comfortable being uncomfortable? You certainly do that when rolling on a call and first encountering a scene. The skills you employ to encounter, analyze, and discern a path of action are the same skills you can use in the presence of the paranormal. The main difference is the obvious...the paranormal is invisible and perhaps inaudible. Your physical senses and fight/flight reactions are heightened but now you are faced with an enemy who appears to have the upper hand.

Why do you feel that fearful uncertainty? The nervous system does not differentiate between excitement and fear, or between a true threat or a false alarm. A ghost does not know that but a demonic being does. How can you create new ways to calm your emotions in the presence of a Presence?

It will call up all of your training as well as your beliefs to respond well. You will react in battle only as well as you trained. Muscle response will repeat what it learned in even when your conscious mind is focused on the immediate threat of shifting

parameters. SO…what if you did some prayerful training before encountering an otherworldly entity or event? Voila...forearmed with the Shield of God may be a handsome addition to your kit.

My choice of prayers and invocations for you were carefully chosen based on my 40 years on the fields of "what

works," as well as a respectful honoring of the variety of religions and spiritual beliefs out there. What works for you

will connect our heart and mind to the comfort of Higher Power. This list of blessings is neither exhaustive nor conclusive. My prayer for you is that I have chosen wisely and with purpose.

But more important than my perspective or practice is YOUR

arsenal of spiritual prayers and invocations to blast light into the

darkness. I chose prayers and invocations with a high attractor pattern, meaning they do not

condemn you for being human...nor do they create guilt or fear

when you are attempting to learn and simply understand, see?

Positive affirmation and reinforcement of the love, light and

power of The Creator is, to me, the strongest medicine for an

ailing world. Enjoy these and trust in your own discernment to

KNOW.

THE GREAT INVOCATION

"The Great Invocation, used by Christ for the first time in June 1945, was released by Him to

humanity to enable us to invoke the energies which would

change our world and make possible the return of Christ and

Hierarchy. This World Prayer, translated into many languages is not sponsored by any group or sect. It is used daily by men and women of goodwill who wish to bring about the right human relations among humanity." (1)

FROM THE POINT OF LIGHT WITHIN THE MIND OF GOD

LET LIGHT STREAM FORTH INTO THE MINDS OF MEN.

LET LIGHT DESCEND ON EARTH.

FROM THE POINT OF LOVE WITHIN THE HEART OF GOD

LET LOVE STREAM FORTH INTO THE HEARTS OF MEN.

MAY CHRIST RETURN TO EARTH.

FROM THE CENTER WHERE THE WILL OF GOD IS KNOWN

LET PURPOSE GUIDE THE LITTLE WILLS OF MEN-

THE PURPOSE WHICH THE MASTERS KNOW AND SERVE.

FROM THE CENTER WHICH WE CALL THE RACE OF MEN

LET THE PLAN OF LOVE AND LIGHT WORK OUT

AND MAY IT SEAL THE DOOR

WHERE EVIL DWELLS.

LET LIGHT AND LOVE AND POWER

RESTORE THE PLAN ON EARTH.

THE LORD'S PRAYER IN ARAMAIC

the language spoken by Jesus, (2)

Our Father in Heaven

Hallowed be Thy name

Thy Kingdom come

Thy Will be done

as in Heaven so on earth.

Give us bread for our needs

from day to day

Forgive us our offenses as we

have forgotten our offenders.

Do not let us enter into

Temptation.

Deliver us from evil

For Thine is the kingdom ... and the power

... and the glory

For ever and ever. Amen

A-voon de-vesh-ma-ya

Nith-ka-dash-smakh

Tai-thai mal-koo-thakh

Neh-wey sev-ya-nakh

Ai-ken-na de-vesh-ma-ya

Up ber-ah, hav-lan

Lakh-ma de-soon ka-nan

Yo-ma-na wush-vok-lan

khoe-baine ai-ken-na de-up

khnan sh-vak-n el-kha-ya-ven

Ula ta-e-lun el nis-yoe-na

II-la pes-on-min-bee-sha

Mit-thil de-de-lakh-ee

Mal-koo-tha oo-khay-la

Oo-tish-boakh-ta

El-a-lum all-meen. A-men.

THE KADDISH

Hebrew: JEWISH Prayer for The Deceased

Yit-ga-dal ve-yit-ka-dash she-me ra-ba

be-al-ma di-ver-ah chi-re-u-tel,

ve-lam-lich mal-chu-tai be-cha-ye-chon,

de chol beit Yis-raeil,

ba-a-ga-la u-vi-ze-man ka-riv,

ve-i-me-ru: a-mein.

Ye-he she-mei ra-ba me-va-rach

le-a-lam u-le-ai-mei al-ma-ya.

Yit-bar-ach ve-yish-ta-bach,

ve yit-pa-ar ve yit-ro-mam ve yit na-sei

ve-yit-ha-dar ve-yit-a-leh ve-yit-ha-lal

she-mei de-ku-shah, be-rich hu,

le-ei-la min kol bi-re-ha-ta, ve-shi-ra-ta

tush-be-cha-ta ve-ne-che-ma-ta

da-a-mi-ran be-al-ma, ve-i-me-ru: A-mein.

I WROTE THESE PRAYERS ESPECIALLY FOR YOU...

I.

Father of Light and love, I call forth your power to stand with me at this time. Shield me with the armor of truth. Guide my mind with your wisdom. Strengthen my emotions with your calm resolve. Oh, Father of my heart, I invoke You in the name of all that is good. Protect me from harm. Sharpen my skills of discernment so that I may face the enemy with Your weapons of brilliant light and confidence. Oh God of my heart, I thank You for Your help. Amen.

II.

I am that I am. My strength cometh from the Lord. There is nowhere He is not. The world is filled with His bounty and goodness and I am a part of that world. My life is in His gentle hands at all times. My thoughts are nowhere if not with Him. I am the strength of the Lord. His mercy and strength endureth forever. Amen.

III.

Oh Lord, I ask for your help in this time of trial. I stand in a web of uncertainty but know You are always with me. Dear God, I fear this trial and ask for our comforting Angels to minister to me. You are my rock and my hope. I am nothing without you. I ask humbly for vision, for courage, for clarity of thought. Oh Lord, thank you for your constancy within my life. Amen.

IV.

Bless the Lord, oh my soul. Bless His life within mine. The Lord is my strength and my willpower. He stands beside me, He stands in front of me, and He stands behind me at all times. I am always within the protective shield of the Lord. And because of it I come to no harm. Amen.

V.

Oh, Father of my heart, fill me with the courage and resolve of your greatest warriors. Enliven my spirit with the longing to do Your work. Strengthen my mind with the brilliance and strategy of Your greatest leaders. Empower my body with the certainty of a thousand battles won. Oh, Father of my heart, I invoke You to make this so. Amen.

VI.

Oh Lord, where shall I find Thee when weakness overcomes my spirit? When my resolve fails and my heart falters in fear, where do I find Thee when I can barely find myself? Oh Lord, help me to see that tiny light in the darkness and know that it is You calling me back. Show me how to wax in strength when all around me wains in hope. Oh Lord, thank you for righting me on the path. May I always remember to call myself back to You. Amen.

VII.

Dearest God, I am yours and You are mine. No one stands between us. Every day is Your day and every night belongs to You. There is no power greater than Yours, no love sweeter and no light brighter than the ethereal presence of You within me. Lord of all, of Heaven and Earth and all that lies therein, I bless You and call You closer to me. In Thy holy presence I remain steadfast in my love for You. Amen.

VIII.

Oh, dearest God, I don't know what has happened. I fear itself. My mind refuses to calm itself and my body shakes in anger. Dearest God, what am I to do? I am at a loss and cannot seem to find You within me. I now affirm that You are always present even in the shadows of my life. I now call myself back to You and resolve to love myself even when I fear and hate and deceive my heart that all is not well. Oh, dearest God, I invoke forgiveness of self. You never judge me, only I myself. Amen.

IX.

The sweetness of the Lord is likened to the ripe fruit in a garden of plenty. The power of the Lord is the towering mountain of pure stone. The wisdom of the Lord cannot be swayed even by the holy hosts. Blessed be the Lord in all things of Heaven and Earth. May His love, light and power reside win me, His servant, forevermore. Amen.

X.

Straight is the path to the presence of God. Deep is the ocean of His love for me. He teacheth me of His ways as I walk the path of His Will for me. Naught am I deterred from His Presence. The lord is my strength and my hope from this time forth and forever more. Amen.

XI.

When my enemy faces me, I will have no fear. May he serve as a mirror of what I have yet to accept. I falter not in my resolve, for joy cometh in the morning light of clear truth. I am the seed of my becoming, planted in the fertile soil of my enemy's challenge. I shall birth my courage from that seed of hope. All is well with me when I remember God.

AMEN, OMEIN, AHO

Welcome To My Paranormal Life

Well, I guess it's time to tell you about some of my own paranormal experiences. If I am paying attention, this stuff is going on 24/7. Most of the time I just tune it out, literally. But others tell me that I have attenuated myself so intrinsically to psi that my life just breathes with it. Fair enough. I don't even recall the first experience I had because one bleeds into the next. But I can relate some of them to give you an idea of how it works in my life so that you can perhaps recognize the signatures in yours.

I am told that I listen well, and that I have trained myself to actually believe what I see and hear as truth where psi is concerned. Clues are the answer. What does that mean? Follow the prompts...one clue will roll over onto the next one in a synchronous fashion. So, it is kind of like a board game where I would look at a clue, make a move and then wait for the next clue to show up. But how does that happen?

I allow myself to remain curious. Curiosity is a value from our childhood that presses us to move foreword with purposeful intent. Intent to do what? To wonder about what comes next and to search it out. Paranormal phenomena are connected by threads of commonalities...when did that occur, to whom, why, and what is the effect of the event upon the environment? We put a lot of our own prejudices, pre-judged opinions, into all situations because of the stress created from new stimuli requiring to be connected to what we know in order

for us to GET IT.

I am constantly scanning my environment for the next clue when on a case or when I become aware of a paranormal event in my personal life. Connecting the dots is a game I play. I will give you an example of my process by relating a recent AH-HA, my term, of course:

My awesome husband's dad passed away in 1993. This thesis is dedicated to him because he keeps showing up to help me. Big Tom was 6' 5" and a Senior Patrolman out of Richmond,

California. I had seen Big Tom's photo in our home but had clearly never met him in the flesh. In November of 2014 I went

down into my husband's Man Cave to take him some lunch and was amazed to see a huge dude sitting in the rocking chair,  smiling at me. No, I was not afraid because I see dead folks daily, but I was clearly shocked because I recognized him as Thom's deceased dad. I mentally asked him what he was doing and he responded that he just showed up occasionally to check up on Thom. I asked him if he could perhaps help me with this thesis as I knew he had been a cop and I needed to understand more of the feeling-tone you guys run through daily.

"Done!" he exclaimed, clapping his huge hands once as he rose out of the rocker. I thanked him and watched the form disappear into a decay pattern.

"Your dad was just here," I told Thom as I walked into his shop area.

"Yeah," he said nonchalantly. "I see him sometimes. I think he's curious about our house."

Over the next four months I began to see and feel him around a lot more. We have become friends and I so regret I missed the honor of knowing him while he was alive. Great guy, great American.

So, last night Thom and I had enjoyed a nice meal with our neighbors at a restaurant in Missoula. As we all walked through the parking lot, I laughed at the clean cars that clearly belonged to folks in town, contrasted with our truck and several other trucks seemingly owned by those living remotely, meaning up a five-mile logging road with 100 ft. drops and no guard rails.

"Wow, that just cracks me up!" I began. "I think I'll start calling city-dwellers flatlanders. I mean, I only wash my truck one in the spring and once in fall because by the time I get up the mountain it is already covered in dirt."

We all laughed at the familiarity of our lives together on the mountain, but I wondered where I got that name because it was an unfamiliar word to me. On the way home, Thom casually remarked, "You know, that is exactly what my dad used to call them."

"Call who?" I asked.

"He called people who lived in town flatlanders." Bingo. Dots connected. Why did Big Tom put that in my head? Dunno but I know he did. It seemed like a loving thing to do, like he was there with us enjoying a beautiful spring evening under the Montana stars.

I am convinced that most paranormal events are innocuous and perhaps as casual as the story I just shared. I have

trained myself to NOT intellectualize, deny, or blow off these subtle gentle clues as they enter my consciousness. You can train yourself to do the same. Remain curious and ask what the situation reminds you of...is there a signature you intuit from a previous event that has laid down tracks or you to follow? Have fun with it and refuse to allow anxiety about the unknown to scare you off. This stuff happens all the time. Spend time with children and animals in God's natural world. Go out into nature and

claim your birthright of blessing your body with sunlight and fresh air. Pay attention and watch your spider senses get even better than they already are from your training and work experience. And guess what? Most of the paranormal events you encounter are NOT awful. They are usually blessings from loved ones or whispers from a distant star. We tend to categorize all of them into the fearful-category, forgetting that God's world can be magnificently gentle and comforting, right?

On that note, let me share a most amazing event with you, one for which I was totally unprepared. OK ...I don't know "the reason why" the other realms appear to seek out my participation, but they do. Whatever. But this event stands out in my mind as truly amazing:

Before moving to this Montana, I had a farm in Washington State. This beautiful place was (and still is) a hot bed of paranormal events. Way cool. One morning after I had fed my fold of Scottish Highland cattle, I felt led to wander around the back of the barn and gaze up the access road toward the "survivor tree." The top of this cedar had broken off years ago and left the tree to survive in that state, which it did quite

well. The farm dogs were constantly rooting out raccoons from the hidey-hole three feet up, while countless times had I walked by two eyes shining in the darkness in that hole. You get the picture.

But this morning, I was to experience something different. As I looked up the road toward the tree, I blinked my eyes because I saw, literally saw, a gnome standing there. What the hell. Look again, yep, still there. I wandered up the road to the tree. There he was, just like you'd see on TV—the garden gnome with the red cap, staff, beard, and gnome clothes.

I recall being completely comfortable at this point. The gnome pointed to the hidey-hole and mentally asked me if I would reach in there. Remember the raccoons? Well, for some reason I was unconcerned because I trusted the little guy. So, I reached about two feet into that dark hole and felt something cold and furry. I grasped it, pulled it out

of the hole and saw it was a dehydrated squirrel. The gnome dude instructed me to put in on top of the old growth cedar stump near the survivor tree, which I did. And then he asked if I would reach in there again. Lo and behold, a second dehydrated squirrel! I placed the second find on the stump next to the first one, wondering the how and why of the situation, but having no doubt that I did the right thing. I turned back to the gnome but he had dematerialized. SO strange.

The next morning, I returned to the tree and saw that the two squirrel carcasses were gone. his may sound strange, but to

this day I wonder more about who took those carcasses than the gnome situation. But this was only the beginning of my

gnome adventures. Enter—Montana.

One morning I got up early and wandered into the bathroom taking time as I love to do, to look out the bathroom window at the magnificent ponderosa pine forest surrounding our home. WHOA! What was that?! A gnome had fully materialized next to a stump on the hillside, about forty feet from the  window. I blinked my eyes, thinking that perhaps I was still asleep, but he was still there. I then got a mental message from his that, "everything will be OK now. The worst has passed."

Truly, I was shocked but comforted. I stood looking at  him for a minute or so, thanked him and watched the form start to waver as he dematerialized. A similar manifestation occurred a month later, but this time he was standing a bit down the mountain toward the gulch. No message that time, but still way cool.

Why does this stuff happen to me? Again, your guess is as good as mine, but I intuit it is partially because I am still a kid at heart, you know? I think that is part of it, if we remain as the

Bible says, like children, perhaps the heaven we experience on Earth can be from the natural world of wonder.

So, what about the icky scary stuff I have encountered? Some of it is from evil forces but the rest is scary because I was being a chicken sh**. For example, this next phenomenon is a

recurring in my life and I have yet to own it. Big ole paranormal investigator, right? You decide.

Three months ago, Thom was gone for the weekend on a fun hunting adventure. I had retired rather early because I wanted to arrive at church early enough to join the prayer circle. I think I had barely drifted off to sleep and felt someone sit down on the side of the bed. The mattress went down as if someone weighing at least one hundred pounds was sitting there. I was laying on my back, about twelve inches from the edge of the bed. It was a distinct signature of a weight lowering the mattress.

I froze—literally stopped breathing—with my eyes clamped shut. This is my M.O. whenever Spirit does this...total coward, right? So, I obviously had to resume breathing but do not recall how long they were there. Was I awake? I intuit I was in an altered state, you know? The next thing I recall was waking up at 7AM and wondering what the heck or WHO that was. Retrograde Courage is the term I call my after-the-fact lock and load reaction to this stuff. NOW I was curious and unafraid.

I fixed a cup of coffee and padded over to my office computer. I took a sip of hot brew, as I looked over my new e mails. I choked on the coffee, spitting the mouthful out over my key board. What did the e mail say?

"The Traditional Martinist Order invites you to apply for membership..." I knew absolutely that I was supposed to join this order. Over my thirty-nine years of membership in the sister school, The Rosicrucian Order, I had never felt drawn to join the Martinists. I guess my orders had just been changed. I felt the presence of the Being who was requesting I pay attention and follow the prompts. And so it

goes. All right, I'm stalling. Writing about the truly evil stuff sucks all the oxygen out of the room. I considered omitting that from this thesis but I know I owe it to you, at least some of the stories. The very worst case I took on was in Nashville in the late 1970s. I was in the process of setting up a

Psychical research center and was teaching psi classes out of my home. A gal contacted me through a student who relayed that "a girl was in an awful situation" and would I talk with her? Sure. To maintain privacy with dates and names I will refer to this girl as "Rita."

Rita called me and told me that her boyfriend was a satanist and she was afraid for her life. He was involved with some black witches outside of Nashville and lots of bad stuff

was going on in her home and to her personally. Rita lived with her two kids in the home he owned. She

agreed to come over the next day to tell me more stuff. Oh joy.

When I opened the door, I was surprised to see a lovely young woman with a beautiful smile, not what I had expected. Rita sat down and pulled up her sleeve, showing me recent 6" scars of upside-down crosses on her forearm. Now, the upside-down cross can be a satanic signature because evil wants

to mimic the cross that John the Baptist chose to be crucified on because he said he was not worthy to be crucified like Jesus. Satanic forces also like to do things opposite to the Church, as they are incredibly stupid and have no singular creativity of their own.

I agreed to do a walk through of the house. When I drove up, I felt that familiar chill up my spine. I knew there were forces at work that did not want me there. Being young and naive I

ignored that and knocked on the door. Rita looked totally freaked but tried to hide it. I could see her satanic boyfriend,

"Odin," sitting in a lounger watching TV. I KNEW he knew why I was there, yet he remained mute.

Obsessed and possessed people cycle in and out of the demons manifesting outwardly, so these demons were hiding from me.

"Those witches know about you and called here to warn me not to let you in." she whispered, as we went into the kitchen and closed the swinging door. If I had had one iota of the intuitive intelligence I own today I would have said, "Yep…call a priest."

Enter moi. The house felt cold and sticky. Something was not right, at least I knew that. Rita gave me a quick tour (looked like a hippie drug house) and kept apologizing for the mess, saying she could never seem to get the place clean. She then took me to the garage and we stopped in our tracks…there on

 the wall was a clear outline of a man holding what looked to be like a Bible.

"Oh!" she exclaimed. "The preacher is back!"

His image on the wall looked like a shadow that was fading in and out and finally disappeared. Rita went on to explain that an African American preacher had befriended her awhile back but had passed on. His spirit had shown up at the home several times and she thought he was the one who got she and I connected. We went back into the house, talked a bit, and decided for her to attend my regular psi class the next night.

During the class I asked Rita if we could do some

hypnosis

to see if

we could

discern how and why the demonic was trying to work in her. The

house they lived in was in the Oppression stage, very dangerous

because the demonic had been able to call in some bigger ones

to start moving things, breaking glass, and scratching upside-

down crosses on poor Rita's arms and back.

Rita proved to be a suggestible subject to hypnotize and

as soon as she went under, the scratches began manifesting on

her arms and lower

neck. That was all the

proof I needed, duh. I

strongly suggested to

Rita that she find some way to exit the home with her kids and

few possessions. Agreed. The plan was that she would call me

when she knew Odin would be gone for a while, allowing us to

get her to a safe location.

A couple of weeks passed while other cases and the normalcy of life created a benevolent amnesia from Rita's

dilemma. But at sunset on a Friday evening, she called me in a panic.

"Odin suspects something...those witches he knows said they were going after 'that girl' and he should not let you back into his house!" she panicked.

I sprung into action, hurriedly telling Rita to pack what she could and I would be there in thirty minutes. True to my twenty-five-year-old no-judgment-centered brain, I rushed over to her place, loaded Rita, her kids and lots of stuff in garbage bags into

my Honda. Rita instructed me to take them to a cabin about forty minutes northeast of Nashville where her cousin would pick them up the next day. I seem to recall the cabin belonged to a

 friend of her former husband. Something like that.

After dropping them off I swore off the paranormal rescue drama...for life. Three months later, Rita called me and invited me to see where they were living. She fed me some wild pigeon and corn bread as a thank you. I have never heard from her since but pray she is safe and well.

So, what other stuff has happened? I will tell you one more thing but will end it with that. If we meet in person,

perhaps you can ask me the right question and coerce me to tell

you more stuff from beyond the veil.

But here's another true tale...

I was living outside of Birmingham, Alabama in the mid 1980s and began a new cycle of research in the paranormal.

During this period Spirit guided me to read books on possession

and really learn more about demonology in preparation for later works. As I have told you, this stuff is awful to read and research. It takes something out of you to soak your days in the swamp of the demonic. I prayed constantly, got baptized again and kept multiple altars around my little home. I continually dedicated my books, papers, home, thoughts, and life to Christ, so I felt loved and protected even when "walking through the valley of the shadow of death." My

belief was that if God wanted me to put myself in hell to learn this stuff so I could help others, then God would keep me safe from demonic attack. And that is exactly what happened. Still does, but His protection does not keep the demonic from showing up to scare the holy crap out of you. And that is what happened one night in my house.

I'll set a scene for you so that you can get a glimpse of the environment I am asked to inhabit. Then, as now, my bed stand holds a cross, a relic form of a particular saint, holy water, a blessed candle, a .357, and a knife. The last two are for the blood and guts monsters. There are always at least ten books on the night stand and next to the bed, romance novels they are not. Back then, some of the research Spirit wanted me to read were *The Exorcist, Messages from Michael, Initiation, Serial Killers, Sociopathology, Crime Classification Manual, The DSM-111, Cannibal Killers, The Psychology*  *of Violence,* and the like. You get the picture. And yes, I slept like a baby. But for the grace of God, my life was protected and healthy.

One evening, after finishing *The Exorcist*, I headed back to my TV room which door always remained closed to preserve  the air conditioning. As I walked down the hall, I heard a weird buzzing that increased in volume as I put my hand on the door knob. When I opened the door, I fell back against the wall...the room was filed with flies, I mean thousands massing against the white walls. Recognizing this as a demonic attack I called out "I cast you from my home in the name of The Lord Jesus Christ and wash my home in the blood of Christ."

I then ran through the awful mess, opened the window, and watched the flies rush out into the night. So, if I

was so protected why and how did that happen? I intuit that the closer we are to the Creator, we can allow more of His light to work and shine through us. That light attracts good and evil like moths to a flame. Or, in this case, flies. When I prayed over that incident, I realized that some stuff slips through the cracks…no harm done but gave me a good scare and a valuable lesson to keep God in front of me at all times.

What I want you to glean from these events is the truth that anything can happen, but God is ever-present. Find a God-centered path and practice it daily. This is your greatest weapon against evil.

Demonomania

An uncomfortable truth:

If you think you have no personal power, you will steal it from others, stand behind movements and throw politically-correct threats when confronted with opinion different from your own. You will wallow in blame and accuse others of taking your power when you have not yet owned yours...warring against them to supposedly get yours back. These are the behaviors of cowards and fools who choose to walk with demonic energy, using it as a shield against their own ignorance. Evil will cajole and tempt you with earthly, temporary power and wait for you on the other side of the darkness. Don't go there.

True evil cannot be talked out of its intent, nor can it be coerced and loved into change. You cannot have a sane conversation with an insane being. It is EVIL, see? It is not a mental disorder or an addiction to be soothed and healed. It hates you and all you represent. Some choose to side with the demonic because they think it will keep them safe. They are cowards. It knows you are vulnerable at that point because you have chosen them over the God they hate. Those choosing that path think that evil is fun and sexy and fashionable. Their free will is gradually, insidiously, and cunningly muted to leave

them with nothing but the silence of their own hell. Fear, pain, depression, boredom, rage, and all their dithering cousins will transform those poor souls into flesh ripe for the taking.

The fallen angel who started the rebellion in Heaven is called Satan. Satan was God's favorite. His brilliant radiance outshone all others, and this was the beginning of the end, before he divorced the Creator of Heaven and Earth. Satan became jealous that God had gifted free will to Humanity, making them "a little lower than the Angels." So, he left with the other rebelling Angels. God gave them Earth for their home. This Earth is still the home of Satanic forces.

How do they get and keep power? The demonic requires humanity as its host. They have no actions except through us, see? They can do nothing by themselves because they have no free will. But guess who does, US! We have the power to choose good over evil. It is as simple as that.

Every choice we make attracts more good or more pain...like attracts like.

This is good news. God's good news. He knows the end from the beginning. Trust and more trust will come to you.

Your Questions

My husband and I are blessed to enjoy the friendship of many in law enforcement. I have asked  several officers to relate several cases involving the paranormal, and to ask me some questions they would like answered.

The first is an officer in Washington State, also a former SWAT cop, and an expert in personal defense a tenured police officer for over twenty-eight years, I have experienced my share of strange occurrences involving people. Some behaviors could easily be explained as being attributed to drugs, alcohol, mental

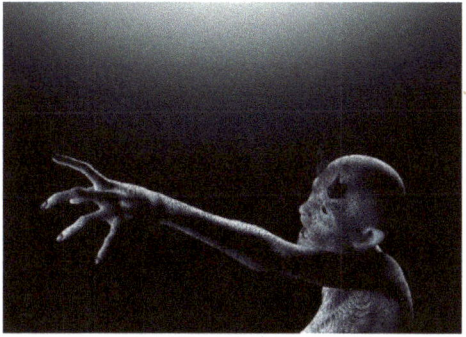

illness, and persons classified as sociopaths. However, I have

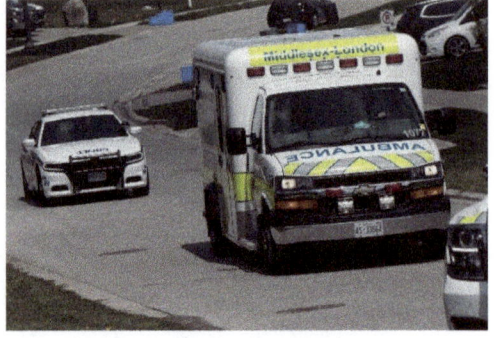

also experienced some things can only be classified as unexplainable. What follows here is the verbatim account from that Sargent in Washington state.

One example involved a family who experienced the loss of a loved one. The woman was found dead, one morning. When a sister of the deceased was told of her death she exclaimed "She told me! She told me!"

Not understanding what she meant, she explained to me that her sister had spoken to her dead mother the night before. She said at first she did not believe her and attributed her sister's statement to her being tired after taking medication. But now she believed that

her dead mother had indeed, possibly because she knew her

daughter was close to death.

Several minutes later I encountered the grandmother of the recently deceased. She was confined to a couch in the family room due to her age and physical impairment. The room was located at the back of the residence. It was isolated from all the activity at the front of the house. At the time, the residence was full of family members, police officers and medical personnel, yet no one had told her of the death of her granddaughter. So, I told her and offered my condolences. Surprisingly, the grandmother seemed at peace with what had occurred. She said she had already been told of her granddaughter's death. She then pointed to a couch

in the room and said that a family member had sat there to tell her. She then told me that person's name.

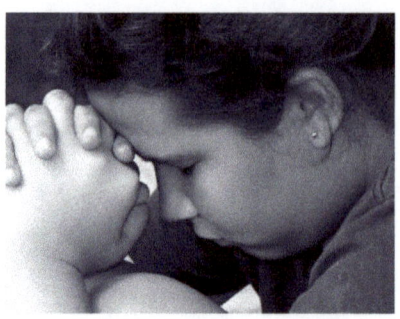

I found all of this odd because I had just asked the others if the grandmother had been told, and they all said she had not. But because the home was so filled with family who were all busy, perhaps someone had not heard what I asked, so I thought little of it at the time. I then went back to the front room where everyone had gathered. I told them that I had notified the grandmother but that she already knew about the death. I remember when I said the name

of the family member who had told her, the entire room fell silent! All the family members had a shocked look o their faces! Several quietly gasped. I naturally wondered what I had said to bring on such a reaction. One of the sons-in-law then revealed that the name was indeed that of the

deceased.

This incident was witnessed by several family members, firefighters and one other police officer. We all experienced a moment of pause during which we silently exchanged glances.

I have investigated many deaths before and since that incident but have never had such a strange and inexplicable occurrence.

Another example involved a call in which a female suspect, without provocation, calmly entered a hair salon while armed with a large butcher knife. She walked up to a customer who was reclined in a chair getting her

hair washed, and plunged the knife into her chest.

All witness accounts said that the female had entered the adjoining grocery store without saying a word, 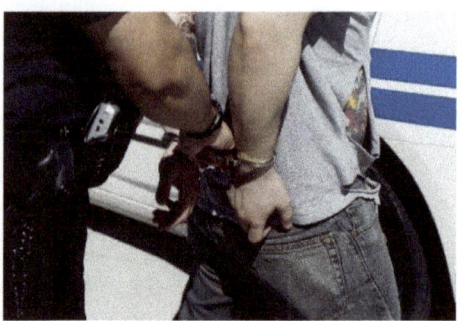 and had purchased the butcher knife. Many described her as having a blank expression on her face, while others described her as mentally ill. When asked why they thought she was mentally ill they replied that it was "just the way she looked."

After stabbing the victim, the subject calmly exited the salon. She was contacted as she aimlessly wandered within yards of that place. She was taken into custody without incident. She would not speak when questioned by officers. The primary officer took a photo of the subject immediately after being taken  into custody, in order to preserve evidence of her clothing and demeanor. When I observed the photo, a chill went down my spine. I can only describe the look on the suspect's face as one of demonic possession. Of course,

she was later declared incompetent to stand trial, due to illness, as she had also been confined to a mental institution prior to

the assault.

I could go on with several other strange incidents but I think you get the point...there are things I have experienced which are so strange as not to be able to be explained.

I don't know how many times I and my fellow officers

have commented prior to a grave shift that we have the feeling it will be a busy night! Being cops, we

often refer to the full moon as being the cause, but I think we do so because we are just not ready to accept that sense of evil, we intuitively feel. We definitely are not usually ready to vocalize that to each other.

But if we were brave enough, for lack of a better word, to examine or question those strange occurrences, what would those questions be?

(end of his stories)

In my humble opinion, I cannot imagine that lack of bravery keeps officers from asking these questions! Perhaps it is simply that the timing is rarely appropriate to delve into the metaphysics of the paranormal when you are rolling up on an armed felony suspect.

Questions from the previous officer:

Q: Is there really such a thing as demonic possession?

A: Yes, even in these modern times such a condition exists. Demonic possession occurs in several instances, yet most agree that it is ALWAYS through invitation, in one form or another. I know of a case where a young woman said she was giving up on God because she did not like her life. She invited Satanic forces into

her life to improve it, which it did on the surface temporarily but she then became gravely ill.

In a case documented by the psychiatrist and paranormal researcher Dr. Scott Peck, a woman became possessed due to her evil mother's influence and her father's avarice. She became like this herself, choosing money over God.

Another of Dr. Peck's cases demonstrates how a gentle naïve girl became possessed seemingly because she was so saintly and evil hated her because of it. In that case, though, I would point to complications from another lifetime which set her up for possession in this one. Strange but true…you just cannot make up the stuff that happens!

True possession is very rare. That is why the Catholic Church maintains strict guidelines to rule out mental illness, fakery, or a physical malady such as seizures which can mimic possession.

Q: Can evil be sensed, like an evil night where you know or sense strongly that something will happen?

A: It seems to me that this fine officer has some paranormal intuition on his duty belt! Yes, absolutely,  *evil IS sensed. It has viscosity…an altered time and space accompanies it, whose signatures are unmistakable once you choose to recognize it. The emotion attached to it is revulsion. Fear comes next. The absolute unnaturalness of evil feels out of place in God's world. It is nothing to get used to or to become complacent and deny its raw awful power. There is nothing decent, kind, good, or worthy about the feeling you will*

 *absolutely get in the presence of evil. Recognize it as The Enemy.*

When you get that feeling that something evil comes your way, pay attention and be on guard that things will not be as they appear.

Demonic forces are masters at deception. They know no truth and will twist you sideways. Forewarned is forearmed.

Q: Do spirits of the recently deceased lurk in a home or place after death?

A: If they died a sudden, tragic, or violent death, yes, they will probably still be there. If the person was very spiritual or evolved, they might just be able to shift out of that emotional state of attachment that holds the others to their past. If the deceased were not evil people, then a deliverance team or clergy specializing in release work can usually send them on their way, but not always. Each case is different and there are lots of

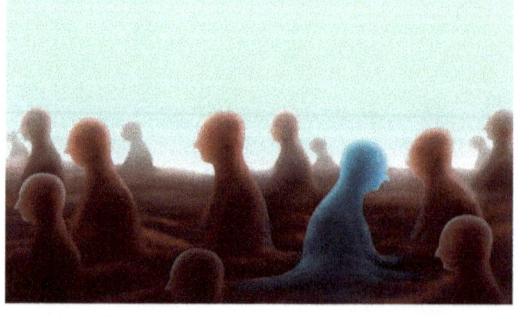

theories on this topic. My personal understanding is that leopards rarely change their spots...if a person was awful in his life, he will be awful when he is dead. Rest assured, though, most folks pass

over and pay little attention to the life they are usually glad to

leave behind...that's why it's called the past!

Q: Do people really have premonitions of their own death, or the death of a loved one?

A: Sometimes they do, but it is not common. Many times, these so-called premonitions are anxiety or false scenarios created from stress of a fertile imagination. Remember that "imagination" can be seen as "image-in-action." Humans are creative souls! But sure, anything is possible. But I think true premonitions about that are rare because we are usually protected from things we may not need to know. Some things are best kept in God's hands.

 *Officer, I hope these answers fill in some spaces for you in your courageous quest for intel on the subject of paranormal phenomena.*

The next set of questions are from a retired Spec. Ops. operator who trains SWAT teams in the Northern regions of the country.

1.) What special handling procedures do you recommend once a possessed person is in custody? i.e. searching and going hands-on with a possessed person...questioning approaches for a possessed person in custody? In custody meaning they are cuffed and disarmed of obvious weapons.

A possessed person in custody would likely be unresponsive with a flat affect, once the demons realize they are in a compromised position.

But remember that possessed folks cycle in and out of the demonic state and their normal consciousness. If the person is also mentally ill, which is often the case, then they may indeed become or remain agitated or violent. Demons are cowards who have no personal power. With no free will or will of their own they are always controlled by the powers above them, meaning the "badder" ones. All demons use threats and intimidations to create fear in their underlings in order to keep them in line.

Demons are stupid and lazy so they get those below them to do the heavy lifting.

A possessed person in custody will be remarkably irritating to handle because you WILL intuit that something nasty has touched you.

Expect to feel revolted and disgusted, impatient, and angry that

you even have to deal with this person. You may wonder later

why all those feelings were surfacing, but have no doubt that they were your defense against the darkness you encountered.

As far as handling, procedure will dictate your processing. It should be determined

by your environment, the crime or infringement committed, and

what you have available to work with. But here's some good

advice...avoid looking in their eyes because you may see

something awful. Physically handle their person as little as

possible and warn the other personnel. It does not matter if they

believe you because later on, they will thank you! Sometimes it takes a

while for the awfulness to sink in and be processed.

Questioning a possessed person could be a routine event if the demons are in retreat, hiding from you knowing they are there. But ask away…you never know.

Any contact with body fluids should be dealt with accordingly. And pray…ask God to step in and assist you, He is always at your side.

2.) Where can I go to actually see, talk to, and interact with possessed persons in order to gain experience, not just reading about it?

You're kidding, right?! Avoid this sh** at all costs. Chances are you will never have to interact with a possessed person because it is so rare. But if you want, YouTube has more than its share of exorcism videos. Most of them are real. I suggest this because it is as close as you can get to this evil without having it slime over your life.

There are actually many Obsessed, not Possessed, people in institutions.
How do you determine who they are? That takes care and time. But here's a really icky fact...the population of those who frequent bars,

casinos, violent faming and the like, are usually in the company of several demonic or dead-spirit beings attached to their body. Addictions create holes in the auric field that God gave you as a shield. All addicts have attachments. The demons or dead folks

can be removed by deliverance teams or those in that field.

But if the addict keeps on keeping on, guess what returns?

And then it is usually much worse because the person has been cleansed and made aware that his free will would have to kick in in order for him to stay clean.

3.) Do possessed people have any natural aversions, such as biblical verses, fire, crosses, holy water, garlic, etc.?

Yes, good question. I'll relate a true story told to me recently by my research partner who was doing some work with a paranormal group in the west. Here is what she said. "One of the gals in our group started dating a man who appeared to be healthy, wealthy, and wise. He drove a fancy car and dressed to the nines.

They had gone out a couple times when he drove her to an area with burn barrels on fire, a desolate place with a weird vibe. He remarked how much he liked all this and asked he is she was drawn to the energy, to which she

forcefully demanded he take her home. He apologized profusely and let her out at her house.

A while afterward, she invited home to accompany her to the home of a couple involved in the paranormal work. They drove to the home, got out of the car, and as they approached the house, he stopped dead in his tracks, refusing to go any further. She asked him what was going on and noticed he was staring at the crosses on the doorpost of the home. He had a frightened look on his face and said he had to leave immediately and that she should come with him.

The gals decided against leaving and let him go on his way. She related that and the burn barrel incident to her friends who were visibly shaken by her story. They told her that those who have been dedicated to Satan, who have done this to themselves, or who are cursed cannot

enter where there are crosses and religious objects. Needless to say, the gal never saw the Satanist again."

In my experience, this is a truth. Jesus Christ gives us

the power and authority to cast out demons IN HIS NAME. To call on the blood of Christ to cast out or cleanse is a potent tool. There are numerous Biblical verses employed by deliverance teams and exorcists. Refer to the Works Cited area of this thesis to learn of some deliverance books available. The Rite OF Exorcism of The Catholic Church is also a powerful tool for a qualified priest-exorcist to use.

For us common folk, prayer, religious items, relics, and blessings can hold back the darkness. Oh, garlic is great in pasta…

But remember this—there are things that are hidden that need to stay that way. Curiosity killed the cat and all that. If you go there, you are in their power center. If you just cannot say no, not even God will interfere with your free-will to dance with the devil. Everything you can imagine exists, maybe not in your immediate reality, but it is out there, believe me.

As a law enforcement professional, I expect you to notice what the general public denies. I also expect you to think long and hard about what I have worked so hard on...to get the point through to you that you ARE prepared by your training to fight whatever you encounter. Believe in yourself and believe in God. You are blessed beyond words.

Contact Information

Rev. Dr. Zoli Althea Browne

3150 Great Northern Avenue

Suite 16868

Missoula, Montana

59808 USA

Phone: 406.499.2163

Email: zoliartexotica@yahoo.com

Website: ZoliArtexoticaMontana.com

Law enforcement professionals and their loved ones are always welcomed to contact me for assistance on a case, or personal concern. All communications will be kept strictly confidential.

Z.

Before, whilst, and after writing Law Enforcement and the Paranormal.

Closing Prayers

The Sword of Cleavage:

Do not think that I came to bring peace on earth. I did not come to bring peace, but a sword. For I have come to set a man against his father, a daughter against her mother, and a daughter-in-law against her mother-in-law, and a man's enemies will be those of his own household. He who loves father or mother more than Me is not worthy of Me. And he who loves son or daughter more than Me is not worthy of Me. And he who does not take his cross and follow after Me is not worthy of Me. He who finds his life will lose it, and who loses his life for My sake, will find it. Matthew 10:34-39

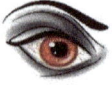

Finally, my brethren, be strong in the Lord and in the power of His might. Put on the whole armor of God, that you may be able to stand against the wiles of the devil.

For we do not wrestle against flesh and blood, but against the principalities, against powers, against rulers of the darkness of this age, against spiritual hosts of wickedness in the heavenly places.

Therefore, take up the whole armor of God that you may be able to withstand in the evil day, and having done all, to stand. Ephesians 6:10-13

I am with you always, even to the end of the age. Amen. Matthew 6:10-13

Thank you, Thom... my warrior and my love eternal.

CITIZEN RIDER WAIVER CLEARANCE FORM

Citizen riders are generally accepted when one or more of the following conditions are met:
- The rider lives in the city limits of ▮▮▮▮   • Lateral Police applicants   ▮▮▮▮ business owners or managers
- The top 10 ranked applicants for entry level police jobs after the oral board   • Officer sponsored citizens

***Per ▮▮▮▮Police Policy 13.4, citizens *(who meet one of the above conditions)* will be cleared to ride ONE TIME only. ***

Citizen riders are approved at the discretion of the Patrol Commander. Officer Sponsored riders may be tentatively approved by Sergeants and then finalized by the Patrol Commander. While officers are being trained or for other logistical reasons citizen riders may not be approved regardless of the general provisions listed above.   Riders will be scheduled on Thursdays or Saturdays for a maximum of four hours unless otherwise approved by the Patrol Commander or his designee.

Full Legal Name: _____ Date of Birth: _____

Alias: *(Maiden Name, Former Name/s)* _____

Drivers License Number: _____ State: _____

Home Address: *(Street, City, State)* _____

Message Phone: (_____) _____ Employer/School: _____

Reason for requesting riding clearance: _____

Have you ever been convicted of a criminal offense (excluding traffic citations)?   ☐ Yes   ☐ No

If yes, please explain: _____

I, _____ *(print your name)*, hereby request permission to ride as a guest of the ▮▮▮▮Police Department in a vehicle owned by the City of ▮▮▮▮ to permit my observation of police work. I understand that should permission be granted, I will be voluntarily observing police work at my own risk and I am willing to assume all risks involved including the risk of death or serious injury. I understand that any information I observe during the Citizen Ride Along experience shall remain confidential unless I am providing information to authorized personnel in the scope and course of an investigation. I also understand that in the event the vehicle in which I am riding becomes involved in a pursuit or other high risk response, at the discretion of the ▮▮▮▮ Police Department, I may be directed to exit the vehicle - regardless of time of day or location, and I am willing to assume all responsibility for my transportation back to the Police Department or to my residence and for any and all harm that may befall me once I exit from the police vehicle.

NOTE: As you will be riding in a confined space, you are asked to cancel your ride if you have a contagious illness, such as flu, cold, fever, etc. Citizen riders must be properly attired with care given to personal hygiene. (Flip-flops/sandals, t-shirts, cutoffs, torn jeans, or careless personal hygiene are not acceptable.)

To the best of my knowledge, I do not have a contagious illness (e.g., flu, cold, fever, etc.) If I do have such an illness develop on or prior to my ride-along, I will cancel the ride-along until such time as the illness has resolved.

WAIVER OF LEGAL LIABILITY

In consideration for granting my request to ride and observe, and being fully aware of the risks involved, I hereby waive any and all legal rights I have or may have in the future, for myself and on behalf of my heirs, to bring any claim or lawsuit against the City of ▮▮▮▮ and its Police Department, individual officers, or any other employees, officers, agents, or volunteers of the City of ▮▮▮▮ arising out of or connected with observing the activities of the ▮▮▮▮ Police Department.

When, in the officer's judgment, it is appropriate to terminate the rider's participation, s/he has the following options:
1. Upon receiving a call, the officer responding to the scene may direct the rider to remain in the patrol vehicle to provide, or call for backup if such is indicated.
2. Upon receiving a call, the officer may pull over to the first convenient and relatively safe location, radio the position of the rider so that another unit can effect a pickup, and proceed to the assignment.
3. A priority rider may bump citizen riders.
4. The duration of ride-along is at the officer's discretion.

Signed: _____ Date: _____

Officer Sponsor: _____ Date: _____

Signed consent of parent or guardian: _____ Date: _____
Required if Citizen Rider is less than eighteen years of age. Minors must be at least 16 years of age or older.

THE PATROL COMMANDER MUST APPROVE ALL CLEARANCE REQUESTS.
IF THIS REQUEST IS APPROVED, YOU WILL BE CONTACTED AT A LATER DATE TO COORDINATE RIDE-ALONG.

Update 04/23/2013 amm

DOCUMENT FROM ONE OF

MY RIDE-ALONGS.

Special Supplement for Officers

As I prepared to send out this work, more questions were presented to me which I deduced would be appropriate to include in a special supplement for officers. It  appears there is no end to the curiosity of many in Law Enforcement for the peculiarities of paranormal experiences! With that in mind, let's take a look at a few more questions:

Q: Is there a difference between a ghost and an  apparition? I heard those terms used on a paranormal show and just wondered what is up with that.

A: True, most of us use the more common phrase of "ghost" to define a spectre or something appearing out of thin air. While the classical ghost is rather disinterested in human interaction, an apparition appears to have something to communicate. Most ghosts are

unaware of your presence because they are stuck in between the

here and there, see?

Many investigators choose not to differentiate between

the two terms, but your question challenged me to root out a

response. In their book published in 2014, Graveyard,

paranormal investigators Ed and Lorraine Warren indeed

differentiate between the two appellations: "Generally, ghosts

are dumb...they stay in the last place they occupied on earth,

they rarely communicate, and they are only occasionally

malicious. Essentially, they are beings that have not resolved all

their earthly sorrows and so now wander around hoping to do

so. (p.29)

"Apparitions are a far different matter. For one thing, they often interact with their earthly host. For another, they frequently have the power to warn earthly friends of dire consequences about to befall them. (p.29)

I usually call those beings ghosts and be done with it. I guess the technicalities can be left up to the parapsychologists and erudite scholars!

Q: I wondered why the ghost shows on TV seem to film mainly at night. Does stuff not happen during the day?

A: Shows are called shows because that is what they are for. Of course, lots occurs during daylight hours. You can actually get some great footage with shadows and light effects that are not present in the dark. The Warrens

report that they got awesome graveyard recordings, on film as well as on tape, during daylight hours. They would allow a simple recording device to run while they perused the grounds, and when played back later on, discarnate voices could be heard on that tape. They also took pictures of gravestones to view faces and symbols that were clearly not there a moment later, although they could see them manifest well enough to mark them for photographing.

Most of my own paranormal experiences occur during the day, perhaps because I am awake to experience them! I see shapes and faces of people as well as critters clearly outlined in

inanimate as well as organic objects, which may or may not be as visible a moment later. Those faces scared the holy hell out of me when I began seeing them around age twenty-one. Now they are a part of my normal

life experience.

These particular manifestations are not "pareidolia"—that is what paranormal investigators label shapes you so commonly see in the clouds. They say that the human mind is constantly: seeking forms we are familiar with...makes sense, but the stuff I see daily often has a communicative signature. I guess you have to make your own call on that one.

Q: How can you be sure you are not making this up? The

mind is really powerful and we can trick ourselves into believing a lot of imaginary stuff. So, how do you know the difference? *A: Excellent question. You don't always know, but with training you will begin to get a feeling about these things, a sixth sense will intrude upon your rational left brain.*

A knowing of sorts accumulates in you so that you get really good, with practice, at discerning what you WANT to believe and what is truly there. That takes some work, but for me, I am

usually surprised at the real stuff and ho-hum about false positives. Granted, I have been practicing since I was about nine years old, so at age sixty-one, I think I got that one down pretty well.

Here is an example of what I mean:

A recent paranormal event in San Antonio exemplifies this training. Over my decades of work in the field of the paranormal, I have diligently trained myself to listen very well, allowing a discernment between the signatures of when something is "me or not

me." I found that the more I truly listen and BELIEVE what I hear, feel, or intuit, the greater became my ability to filter out imagination from the signature of the paranormal. It's like playing the childhood game of curiously wondering what can

happen next...to allow that playfulness to fill the spaces and just be with it, so to speak...try it!

My husband and I were staying at the Hotel Valencia in San Antonio, Texas. Whenever I settle into a guest room I greet and honor the beings in that place by saying a few words to them and offering a prayer. I warmly invite those of good intent to speak with me. At this hotel, I received an image of a middle-aged man dressed in working class clothing from perhaps the early 1900s. He sported a large salt and pepper handlebar mustache, a cap covering the same color hair, and a short brown jacket with similar colored pants.

He was friendly, smiling and a bit surprised that I could see him. "My name is Angelo," he began, "and I lived here and

ran people up and down this river." I got an image of him as a gondolier. I saw him being happy on the river and in his life.

I told my husband what I had intuited, never doubting Angelo's words or my experience of him. But several years ago, I would have doubted myself while attempting to logically explain it as perhaps a fertile imagination, see? Over the last

three years have worked with myself to differentiate between the intuitive signals of a paranormal event

and my own ego wanting to create a drama. With practice you

 can absolutely ascertain the same signals for yourself.

The next morning my husband and I were sitting in the waiting area on the second floor of the hotel, chatting and planning our day. I happened to turn around in my seat to greet a little girl who as dressed festively, and glanced up at the wall behind us.

"Wow, would you look at that!" I exclaimed to my husband.

 There on the wall was hung a full-sized gondola boat. I then heard the gondola ghost say, "My house was here and I still love it."

Ghostly beings are always attached to objects, places, or people. I have rarely been anywhere that I have not met a spirit *of some sort, be it an animal, a ghostly being or even a demonic force attempting to irritate me.*

Something I did not address in the body of the thesis is that you yourself may be mediumistic. Many people are not aware of this and find that they are bothered by spirits or have an ability to intuit things others people just don't get. Self-doubt and feeling silly accompany this ability when it is not understood or accepted by perhaps you or others. Maybe someone in your family, a friend or co-worker has this gift. It is helpful then to realize these skills are perfectly natural but have been pushed to the side or just ignored due to a lack of interest or understanding.

Biographical Material

Diplomas...

1980 University of Science

and Philosophy

1991 Usuru Reiki Master

Degrees...

1974 Stephens Collège AA

1980 U Sci and Philosophy diploma

1991 Usuru Reiki Master degree

2012 Esoteric Interfaith Theological Seminary BA Spiritual

Intuition

2013 Esoteric Interfaith Theological Seminary MA Mystical

Creatures

2014 University of Metaphysical Sciences BA Metaphysical

Sciences

2015 Esoteric Interfaith Theological Seminary Paranormal

Research

2015 University of Metaphysical Sciences M.Sc.

2018 Esoteric Interfaith Theological Seminary DDiv

2017 Esoteric interfaith Theological Seminary PhD Sacred Music

2019 Esoteric Interfaith Theological Seminary PhD Consciousness Research

Ordinations...

2012 Intuitive Minister, Esoteric Interfaith Church

2014 Metaphysical Minister, Esoteric Interfaith Church

2014 Mystic Minister, Esoteric Interfaith Church

2015 Metaphysical Minister, Wisdom of the Heart Church,

2014 Founding Church Charter, Missoula, Montana

"Church Of the Golden Shadow"

Rev. Dr. Zoll Althea Browne, Minister

repressed in the masses of humanity.

-Zoli

YOUR NOTES: _____

_____

_____

_____

_____

FOOTNOTES

"The Emotional Ghost"

1.Mc Clelland, Norman C. THE ENCYCLOPEDIA OF REINCARNATIONAL KARMA, p.32.

2.Myers, F.W.H. (1903) Human personality and its survival of death. London: Longman's Wikipedia.

3.Mead, THE DOCTRINE OF THE SUBTLE BODY IN WESTERN MEDICINE, Watkins, 1919.

4.Plato, THE REPUBLIC. Translated by Desmond Lee, Harmondsworth. Wikipedia.

"Measuring Your Courageous Will"

1.Sarchie, Ralph. DELIVER US FROM EVIL, p. 97.

2.ibid. p. 96.

3.De Becker, Gavin. THE GIFT OF FEAR, p.41.

4.ibid. p.42.

5.opcit. p.44.

"Mirror, Mirror on The Wall"

1.Hungler, SPIRITUAL SURVIVAL FOR LAW ENFORCEMENT, p.i(2)

2.ibid p.ii.

3.opcit p.68.

"That Thing Called Death"

1.Creme, Benjamin. MAITREYA'S MISSION VOL. III., p.559.

2.ibid p.559.

3.opcit p.560.

"Blessings And Prayers"

1.Creme, Benjamin. MAITREYA'S MISSION VOL. III., p.683.

2.Lamsa, Dr. George, THE MODERN NEW TESTAMENT FROM ARAMAIC. p.vi-vii.

WORKS CITED

RECOMMENDED READING

Allen, Thomas B. POSSESSED; THE TRUE STORY OF AN EXORCIST. New York: Doubleday, 1993.

Amorth, Fr. Gabriele. AN EXORCIST TELLS HIS STORY. San Francisco: Ignatius, 1999.

Amorth, Fr. Gabriele. AN EXORCIST; MORE STORIES. San Francisco: Ignatius, 2000.

Baglio, Matt. THE MAKING OF A MODERN EXORCIST. New York: Doubleday, 2000.

Barnstone, Willis & Meyer, Marvin. THE GNOSTIC BIBLE. Boston: Shambhala, 2003.

Bamberger, Bernard. FALLEN ANGELS; THE SOLDIERS OF SATAN'S REALM. New York: Barnes & Noble, 1995.

Beeson, Ray. THE REAL BATTLE: UNDERSTANDING THE DARKNESS. Wheaton: Tyndale,1988.

Belanger, Michelle. THE DICTIONARY OF DEMONS; NAMES OF THE DAMNED. Woodbury: Llewellyn, 2010.

BOOK OF MORMON; ANOTHER TESTAMENT OF JESUS CHRIST. Salt Lake City: Church of Latter Day Saints, 1987.

Buckland, Raymond. BUCKLAND'S BOOK OF SPIRIT COMMUNICATION. St. Paul: Llewellyn,1993.

Charles, R.H. THE BOOK OF ENOCH. Escondido: Book Tree,1999.

Clavell, James. SUN TZU; THE ART OF WAR New York: Delacort,1983.

Creme, Benjamin. MAITREYA'S MISSION VOL.III. London, Share International, 1997.

Davidson, Gustav. DICTIONARY OF ANGELS; INCLUDING THE FALLEN ANGELS. New York: Macmillan, 1967.

Dean, Det. Sergeant Ingrid P. TRUE POLICE STORIES OF THE STRANGE AND UNEXPLAINED. Woodbury: Llewellyn, 2011.

De Becker, Gavin. FEAR LESS; THE REAL TRUTH ABOUT RISK, SAFETY, AND SECURITY IN A TIME OF TERRORISM. New York: Random House, 2002.

De Becker, Gavin. THE GIFT OF FEAR; AND OTHER SURVIVAL SIGNALS THAT PROTECT US FROM VIOLENCE. New York: Random House, 1997.

Delaporte, Father. THE DEVIL: DOES HE EXIST? AND WHAT DOES HE DO? Rockford: Tan Books, 1982.

Denning, Hazel M. PhD. HAUNTINGS! REAL LIFE ENCOUNTERS WITH TROUBLED SPIRITS. New York: Barnes& Noble, 1996.

Douglas, John & Olshaker, Mark. OBSESSION. New York: Scribner, 1999.

Ebon, Martin. THE DEVIL'S BRIDE; EXORCISM PAST AND PRESENT. New York: Harper & Row, 1974.

Eckhardt, John. PRAYERS THAT ROUST DEMONS AND BREAK CURSES. Lake Mary: Charisma House, 2010.

Ehrman, Bart D. LOST SCRIPTURES; BOOKS THAT DID NOT MAKE IT INTO THE NEW TESTAMENT. New York: Oxford, 2003.

Epstein, Pearl. KABBALAH; THE WAY OF THE JEWISH MYSTIC. Boston: Shambhala, 2000.

Fortea, Fr. Jose Antonio. INTERVIEW WITH AN EXORCIST; AN INSIDER'S LOOK AT THE DEVIL, DEMONIC POSSESSION, AND GTE PATH TO DELIVERANCE. Westchester: Ascension Press, 2006.

Freud, Sigmond. THE INTERPRETATION OF DREAMS. New York: Macmillan, 1913.

Friedman, Rabbi Cary A. SPIRITUAL SURVIVAL FOR LAW ENFORCEMENT. Linden: Compass Books, 2005.

Gagnon, Philip. DELIVER US FROM EVIL: A MANUAL OF EXORCISM. Minncapolis: Kirk House, 2008.

Goodwyn, Melba. GHOST WORLDS; A GUIDE TO POLTERGEISTS, PORTALS, ECTO-MIST, SPIRIT BEHAVIOR. Woodbury: Llewellyn, 2007.

Greer, John Michael. MONSTERS: AN INVESTIGATOR'S GUIDE TO MAGICAL BEINGS. Woodbury: Llewellyn, 2001.

Guilley, Rosemary Ellen. HARPER'S ENCYCLOPEDIA OF MYSTICAL & PARANORMAL EXPERIENCE. New York: Harper Collins, 1991.

Haggart, G. P. HOW TO BE A DEMONOLOGIST. USA: Create Space, 2011.

Haggart, G.P. MECHANICS OF DEMONOLOGY. Coleman: Blue Lion, 2009.

Haggart, G. P. SCREECH OWL; THE LIE BEHIND LILLITH. Raleigh: Lulu Press, 2009.

Henning, W B. THE BOOK OF GIANTS; THE FALLEN ANGELS AND THEIR GIANT SONS. San Bernadina: Popular Classics, 2012.

Bungler, David R. M.D. PhD. POWER VS. FORCE; THE HIDDEN DETERMINANTS OF HUMAN BEHAVIOR. New York: Hay House, 1995.

Hungler, Sergeant Craig. SPIRITUAL SURVIVAL FOR LAW ENFORCEMENT. Linden: Compass Books, 2005.

Irine, Alex. THE SUPERNATURAL BOOK OF MONSTERS, SPIRITS, DEMONS & GHOULS. New York: Harper Collins, 2007.

Jung, C. J. THE ARCHETYPES AND THE COLLECTIVE UNCONSCIOUS. New York: Princeton U. Press, 1969.

Kaplan, Matt. THE SCIENCE OF MONSTERS; THE ORIGINS OF THE CREATURES WE LOVE TO FEAR. New York: Scribner, 2012.

Keesling, Dee. NO LONGER HELPLESS; A TRUE STORY OF A MODERN EXORCISM. Kirkwood: Impact Christian Books, 2003.

Kerik, Bernard B. THE LOST SON: A LIFE IN PURSUIT OF JUSTICE. New York: Harper Collins, 2001.

Kovach, Sue. HIDDEN FILES: LAW ENFORCEMENT'S TRUE CASE STORIES OF THE UNEXPLAINED AND PARANORMAL. Chicago: Contemporary Books, 1998.

Larson, Bob. LARSON'S BOOK OF SPIRITUAL WARFARE. Nashville: Thomas Nelson, 1999.

Lamsa, Dr. George. THE MODERN NEW TESTAMENT FROM ARAMAIC. Martinez: Aramaic Bible Society, 2001.

Lhermitt, Jean. TRUE OR FALSE POSSESSION; HOW TO DISTINGUISH THE DEMONIC FROM THE DEMENTED. Manchester: Sophia Institute, 2013.

Mack, Carol and Dinah. A FIELD GUIDE TO DEMONS, FAERIES, FALLEN ANGELS, AND OTHER SUBVERSIVE SPIRITS. New York: Arcade, 1998.

Mandino, Og. THE CHOICE. New York: Bantam, 1986.

Martin, Malachi. HOSTAGE TO THE DEVIL; THE POSSESSION AND EXORCISM OF FIVE LIVING AMERICANS. New York: Reader's Digest Press, 1976.

Mercatante, Anthony S. GOOD AND EVIL IN MYTH AND LEGEND. New York: Barnes and Noble, 1978.

Montgomery, John Warwick, Editor. DEMON POSSESSION; A MEDICAL, HISTORICAL, ANTHROPOLOGICAL AND THEOLOGICAL SYMPOSIUM. Minneapolis: Bethany House, 1976.

Murrell, Conrad. PRACTICAL DEMONOLOGY: TACTICS FOR DEMON WARFARE. Sand Springs: Grace and Truth Books, 2008.

Navarro, Joe. WHAT EVERY BODY IS SAYING; AN EX-FBI AGENT'S GUIDE TO SPEED READING PEOPLE. New York: Harper Collins, 2008.

Nickell, Joe and Fischer, John F. CRIME SCIENCE METHODS OF FORENSIC DETECTION. Lexington: Univ. Press of KY.,1999.

Olson, Dr. Ken. EXORCISM, FACT OR FICTION? Nashville: Thos. Nelson, 1992.

Pagels, Elaine. THE ORIGIN OF SATAN. New York: Random House, 1995.

Peck, Dr. M. Scott. GLIMPSES OF THE DEVIL; A PSYCHIATRIST'S PERSONAL ACCOUNTS OF POSSESSION' EXORCISM AND REDEMPTION. New York: Free Press of Simon & Schuster, 2005.

Peck, Dr. M. Scott. PEOPLE OF THE LIE; THE HOPE FOR HEALING HUMAN EVIL. New York: Simon & Schuster, 1983.

Richards, Larry. EVERY GOOD AND EVIL ANGEL IN THE BIBLE. Nashville: Thos. Nelson, 1998.

Samenow PhD, Stanton E. INSIDE THE CRIMINAL MIND. New York: Random House, 1984.

St. Augustine. CITY OF GOD. New York: Doubleday, 1958.

Sarchie, Ralph & Cool, Lisa Collier. DELIVER US FROM EVIL. New York: St. Martin's Griffin, 2001.

Scott, Bill. THE DAY SATAN CALLED; A TRUE ENCOUNTER WITH DEMON POSSESSION AND EXORCISM. New York: Faith Words, 2001.

Summers, Montague. THE HISTORY OF WITCHCRAFT AND DEMONOLOGY. Mineola: Dover, 2007.

Swope, Pastor. AN EXORCIST'S FIELD GUIDE TO BLESSINGS, CONSECRATIONS, AND THE ERADICATION OF MALEVOLENT ENTITIES. San Bernadino: Open Gate, 2009.

Trimm, Dr. N. Cindy. THE RULES OF ENGAGEMENT, VOL III. SATAN' S WEAPONS EXPOSED. Lake Mary: Creation House, 2006.

Turner, Alice K. THE HISTORY OF HELL. New York: Harcourt, 1993.

Unger, Merrill F. BIBLICAL DEMONOLOGY; A STUDY OF SPIRITUAL FORCES AT WORK TODAY. Grand Rapids: Kragel, 1994.

Ward, Lynd. GOD'S MAN; A NOVEL IN WOODCUTS. New York: Plimpton, 1929.

Warren, Ed & Lorraine. GHOST HUNTERS. New York: St. Martin's Press, 1989.

Warren, Ed & Lorraine. GRAVEYARD. New York: St. Martin's Press, 1992.

Warren, Ed & Lorraine. IN A DARK PLACE. Los Angeles: Graymalkin Media, 2014.

Warren, Ed & Lorraine. SATAN'S HARVEST. New York: St. Martin's Press, 1990.

Warren, Ed & Lorraine. WEREWOLF. New York: St. Martin's Press, 1991.

Whyte, H. A. Maxwell. A MANUAL ON EXORCISM. Springdale: Whitaker House, 1974.

Wilkinson, Bruce. THE PRAYER OF JABEZ; BREAKING THROUGH TO THE BLESSED LIFE. Colorado Springs: Multnomah Books, 2000.

Wilson, Colin. THE OCCULT: A HISTORY. New York: Barnes & Noble Books, 1995.

Young, Wm. Paul. THE SHACK: WHERE TRAGEDY CONFRONTS ETERNITY. Newbury Park: Windblown Media, 2007.

Zalar. ZOLAR'S ENCYCLOPEDIA OF ANCIENT AND FORBIDDEN KNOWLEDGE. New York: Arco, 1984.

Acknowledgements

Thank you to the collaborators who helped in the creation of this book.

Images:

Dreamstime.com

Design:

Linda Beaulieu is a writing consultant and project manager who loves collaborating and helping people share their stories.

Contact her at: lindasusanbeaulieu@gmail.com

Formatting and cover:

Trisha Fuentes is a Top-Rated Freelancer on Upwork who offers book formatting and custom book cover design.

Contact her at: ardentartistbooks@gmail.com

Disclaimer

These writings and the content of this book are the property of Zoliart Companies, LLC, its affiliated organizations and governing bodies, their members, managers, employees, agents or representatives (collectively, the "Owner") and represent the Owner's personal experiences and opinions. These writings and the

content of this book are subject to copyright and may not be sold, transferred, copied, used, or reproduced in whole or in part without the prior written consent of the Owner.

These writings and the content of this book are neither legal, religious, medical, psychiatric, or psychological advice in any way, nor should they be interpreted as such if the reader chooses to adopt and employ any methods presented in this book. The information provided herein is general and not intended to address any specific issue or topic. The accuracy and completeness of information provided herein are not guaranteed or offered to produce any results, and the advice and strategies contained herein may not be appropriate for any one particular person or situation. The Owner shall not be liable for any loss incurred as a consequence of the application or use, directly or indirectly, of any information presented in these writings. The Owner is not responsible for the actions or

failures of any third parties, nor is the Owner responsible for any advertisements or for any content linked to this book. The Owner makes no representation regarding the reliability of this book. Readers accept all risks. Any claim for damages shall be limited to the amount paid by the claimant to the Owner for services.